Return to Palm Island

Return to Palm Island

Bill Rosser

Aboriginal Studies Press
Canberra
1994

FIRST PUBLISHED IN 1994 BY

Aboriginal Studies Press for the Australian Institute of Aboriginal and Torres Strait Islander Studies,
GPO Box 553, Canberra ACT 2601.

The views expressed in this publication are those of the author and not necessarily those of the Australian Institute of Aboriginal and Torres Strait Islander Studies.

The publisher has made every effort to contact copyright owners for permission to use material reproduced in this book. If your material has inadvertently been used without permission, please contact the publisher immediately.

© BILL ROSSER 1994

Apart from any fair dealing for the purpose of private study, research, criticism or review as permitted under the Copyright Act, no part of this publication may be reproduced by any process whatsoever without the written permission of the publisher.

NATIONAL LIBRARY OF AUSTRALIA CATALOGUING-IN-PUBLICATION DATA:

Rosser, Bill, 1927- . Return to Palm Island.
ISBN 0 85575 244 0.
1. Rosser, Bill, 1927- . [2.] Aborigines, Australian — Biography. [3.] Aborigines, Australian — Queensland — Government relations. [4.] Aboriginal Australian stockmen — Queensland — Biography. 5. Ranches — Queensland. 6. Palm Island (Qld). I. Title.
305.8991509436

3000/12/94

PRODUCED BY Aboriginal Studies Press
TYPESET IN Goudy Old Style 10/12
PRINTED IN AUSTRALIA BY Australian Print Group, Maryborough, Victoria.

COVER PHOTOGRAPHS Palm Island, 1962 (photograph Colin Tatz, courtesy AIATSIS)

Contents

Introduction	vii
Chapter 1	1
Chapter 2	9
Chapter 3	19
Chapter 4	25
Chapter 5	35
Chapter 6	39
Chapter 7	51
Chapter 8	67
Chapter 9	79
Chapter 10	83
Chapter 11	107
Chapter 12	111
Chapter 13	113
Chapter 14	119
Chapter 15	135
Epilogue	143
Addendum	147

Introduction

It had been quite some years now since I had strolled the forests and beaches of Palm Island. I have fond memories of the times I played and joked with the kids there and, yes, I have memories of difficulties we faced there, too. But there was never any doubt that I would, some day, return to Palm Island to renew associations with my many friends there. However, my return came about in a most unexpected manner.

Rick, the son of my very dear friend the late Fred Clay, a previous Chairman of the Aboriginal Council on the island, phoned me at my home in Brisbane. He had followed in the footsteps of his father by being elected Chairman of the Palm Island Aboriginal Council. He had managed the task very well but now he was in trouble; he was having difficulties in his work because of apparent faction fighting. He needed my help in setting up a local newsletter on the island, similar to the newsletter which his father and I published in 1974. Of course, I was honoured for my services to be thus required and I suppose I felt perhaps a little smug about the request. I knew I would have no problem in doing the job because his father, Fred, and I used the newsletter to fight the Queensland State Government for the repeal of the Queensland *Aborigines Act 1971*. So belligerent did we become over the issue that, in 1974, we were thrown off the island, which, under the Act, they could legally do.

I was anxious to respond to Rick's call for assistance and it took me very little time to pack a bag and head for the airport, bound for Palm Island.

It was good to be on Palm Island once more; to feel the fine, white sand filter through my toes as I wandered along its beaches. As I stood there, gazing across the dark blue waters towards the mainland, I could see the white shapes of the wild goats feeding on the steep inclines of Fantome Island, one of the islands which make up the Palm Islands group. I could see the tall, slender coconut palms bend gently in the breeze and I fancied they were waving a welcome to me. Palm Island is indeed a beautiful place.

Having said that, one is reminded of the adage: 'Beauty is only skin deep'. How true it is, for beneath the facade of pulchritude lay a community of bewilderment and despair brought about by the adversities of the past. Undoubtedly, the greatest disparagement was brought about by a series of Queensland Aboriginal Acts, the first of which was the *Aboriginal Protection and Restriction of the Sale of Opium Act* introduced in 1897 (amended in 1901). This particular Act was repealed and in 1939 the *Aborigines Preservation and Protection Act* was gazetted. The very words 'Preservation' and 'Protection' were misnomers! It was this particular Act which was the catalyst for the fall and decline of Aboriginal culture for, under the terms of this Act, Aborigines were no longer permitted by law to engage in any manner of their 40,000 years customs or culture! At this stage, of course, Palm Island was still a penal settlement and Aborigines of differing tribal cultures and customs — and both sexes — were thrown together and forced to live under impossible conditions. Under the conditions of this Act, Aborigines were subjected to more oppression than ever. For instance, in order to leave the reserve, written permission by the manager was necessary. The same condition applied for their return (Section 22, clause 1).

Under Section 22, clause 4, an Aborigine — man, woman or child — could be forcibly removed from the reserve. There were more than 120 such sections and clauses in the Act and its Regulations. However, the most diabolical section of all was Section 21, clause 1. It was this section under which the carrying-out of tribal customs and culture (tribal dancing (corroborees), initiation ceremonies, marriage ceremonies or any other 'native practices') was forbidden under threat of imprisonment! Section 21, clause 2 of the Act states: 'Every Aboriginal who disobeys an order of the protector or superintendent to cease dancing [corroborees] and/or other native ceremonies [initiation ceremonies etc] shall be guilty of an offence.'

These sections were well policed throughout Queensland because in country towns the appointed 'protector' was the local police. This particular Act was replaced by subsequent Acts, the last of which was repealed only in 1984. But the damage to Aboriginal society had already been done and no amount of 'Aboriginal Welfare' grants or 'Community Services' grants will ever undo the damage. The plain truth is, because of the ignorance and the fatuousness of white society, Aboriginal customs and culture are gone forever!

I make no apology for my words. Unfortunately, racial discrimination is still rife in many parts of Australia. It is my dream to see an end to racism, particularly in schools because I believe that is where ostracism and prejudice towards our fellow man often consolidate and thereby allow ignorance to overcome compassion.

Chapter 1

I was brought up in the small Queensland country town of Toogoolawah. It was in a largely farming district, both dairy and agricultural, and the farmers were, in the main, of German extraction, many of them actually born in Germany. I didn't have many friends at school; they somehow seemed to shun my friendship and I was too young and unworldly to know why, though all the signs were there. 'Hey, Darkie. You've got spuds in your pants!' This was the usual greeting I got each day as some smart-arse kid laughed and pointed a white, fleshy finger at my patched backside. It was a crude way of letting me know, even at that age, that I was a second-class citizen. A nigger. Actually, the kids went further than merely to boycott me; often they wouldn't even drink from the same tap as me, or wash their hands in the same sink. But things would get back to normal next day: they'd drink out of 'my' tap provided I hadn't drunk from it first. I used to stuff them right up though. I'd go along the row of taps and drink from each of them. The kids would give me a shitty look and then, pulling a face, would condescendingly cup their hands and drink from *that* tap too. I did the same with the wash trough.

The teachers, too, were a captious lot. If anything went wrong or if anything went missing, it was my fault. I spent much of my school time either picking up papers around the yard or just standing outside the classroom door. My nickname was 'Molky' because my mother had married a German called Molkentein. I had a fight just about every afternoon, after school. Invariably, one of the kids would fancy himself and call me names. Of course, I bit and the kid would challenge me to a fight. I don't know why they bothered because I was a solidly built boy and I used to belt shit out of them; but they never learned. Why I was such a solid boy I don't know, because during those days of the depression, my main diet consisted of bread and dripping, or bread and molasses. But I had no difficulty in throwing my adversary onto his back and sitting on his stomach, before proceeding to belt the living daylights out of him. The defeated kid would go home bawling like a lost calf. Next thing I knew, his mother would be on our doorstep complaining to my mother about the way in which I'd thumped her precious little darling.

'He's got a cut eye and his nose is all bleeding,' I remember hearing one woman complain.

'Well,' Mum defended me, 'your boy called my boy names. You should tell him to stop it.' They would argue on for a while but there was never anything the battered boy's mother could do about it. Naturally, I'd be hauled up to the headmaster's office the following day and, after a few well-chosen insults from him and a warning not to fight, I'd cop six of the best on the open palm of my hand. 'The cuts', we used to call them. However, it obviously did no good because, sure as eggs, I'd be down behind the sports pavilion the same afternoon, thrashing some kid again. As I said before, they never learned. As for the patches in the seat of my pants, I was lucky to *have* any pants. We had no money for clothing and I had to go around to the secretary of the local Country Women's Association and ask her if she had any old clothes. I usually ended up with a pair of cast-off trousers — always blue serge — and Mum would cut them up and make a pair of pants for me. She sewed them by hand and, with the greatest respect to my mother, they looked ghastly.

The German bloke Mum had married was a lousy bastard. He would go off to the bush, timber-felling for a week, but before he left he would tell the local grocer and the butcher not to give Mum any credit. I'll never forget the night we went for a walk downtown and ended up outside the local fruiterer where, stacked upon the counter, was a pile of bananas. Mum looked around and, seeing nobody in sight, slipped into the shop and nicked a handful and gave them to me.

'Go for your bloody life!' she said to me. Well, I took off up the street with this handful of bananas and I didn't stop until I got home where I had horrible visions of Mum being lumbered by the police. I could visualise her crying in jail. I began to breathe again only when I heard her thumping up the steps. I peered out to make sure there were no police with her. I was shaking with fright but we sure enjoyed those bananas. For the next few days I wasn't game to go anywhere near that fruit shop.

I can remember clearly, even today, the time we had absolutely nothing in the house to eat. The old man had, as usual, gone off to the bush and left us with nothing. Mum and I went down to the police station and told the sergeant we were broke and had no food. She told him how that mongrel of a stepfather had gone off to the bush and left us destitute. The sergeant said a few uncomplimentary words about him and then gave Mum a piece of paper which she presented at the grocer shop in return for a few items of food. I discovered this was called 'rations'. That night we had the feed of our lives.

Occasionally we had a bit of luxury when a neighbour paid me sixpence for chopping the chips she needed to light her stove in the mornings. Then I'd go down to the butcher shop and get tuppence worth of 'bones for the dog'. The butcher would hand me a huge parcel of bones, but not before I swore for him. His name was Otto Granzien — he used to teach me to swear.

'Say "shit",' he would urge me as he leaned over the counter, grinning like a Cheshire cat.

'Shit,' I would oblige, and the butcher would roar with laughter. If there were any other customers in the shop they would just about piss themselves, too.

That night I would creep out to some farm and pinch some potatoes and whatever else I could see — perhaps a pumpkin — and Mum would make the biggest, richest, thickest pot of soup you ever saw. At times like these we couldn't have cared less if that miserable old bastard ever came home from the bush.

I usually spent the remainder of my 'pay' on a comic — *Mandrake the Magician*, which cost tuppence — and a pennyworth of boiled lollies. Mum would read the comic to me while we both munched on the luxurious sweets.

When I was about six years old, a carnival came to Toogoolawah. It had a merry-go-round; a chairoplane; a strength machine — a device which, if thumped hard enough with a hammer, caused a bell to ring at the top; fairy floss; and all sorts of other things. We kids had never seen anything like it before, and stood goggle-eyed at all the excitement. One of the showmen asked me if I knew anyone who took in washing; I nominated Mum. I'm buggered if I knew if she was interested or not, but the bloke was offering three shillings — a lot of money in those days — and Mum sure needed money. Anyway, Mum did the washing for this bloke — but when he came to collect his nicely washed and ironed clothes, he put the hard word on her. I remember to this day what that sleazy bastard said to my mother: 'If you send that boy away for a while and take me into your bedroom, I'll pay you double'.

Well, Mum didn't muck about; there was this huge pumpkin sitting on the table (I had pinched it the night before). She picked it up and slammed it down on the lecher's head. As the pumpkin rolled onto the floor, this joker let out a bloodcurdling scream, then recovered his balance and, holding his head between his hands, did the four-minute mile out the gate, not bothering about his nicely pressed shirts. Mum still had those shirts years later.

One day my stepfather told us the block of timber he'd been working on had cut out and that he and his mate would have to go further into the bush to where a new stand was available. That meant it would no longer be practical for him to keep coming back home to Toogoolawah each week. So we all packed up and went out bush with him in a sulky. It took two days to get there. We picked out a suitable camping site, then put up the tent and organised a galley over which Mum had to do the cooking.

I was now just eleven years old but, with no transport to take me to school in Somerset Dam, the nearest township, and no mail service to deliver correspondence lessons, my schooling days were over. I wanted to read but could scarcely manage three-letter words and my writing was hopeless. But I loved the bush; I thrived on it. I passed a lot of the time away by going up the scrub with old Tom Doyle, the bullock driver, and, with the help of an enormous whip the bullocky had given me, I soon became quite proficient at handling bullocks. The whip was about thirty-feet long and I learned to crack it. What a thunderous noise it made! The working bullocks certainly took notice when they saw me approaching with this wicked instrument casually hanging from my shoulder, its lash dribbling along the track like a black snake.

One day the timber-truck driver told me that there was a job going on a dairy farm. So I went back with him to see the prospective employer who was only too eager to give me a start. He promised to pay me five shillings a week and keep. I started the next morning: my introduction to the working class.

What a job! I had to get out of bed at 3 am to bring in the cows. I will never forget how my bare feet felt as they broke through the frozen grass. But first I had to catch the horse, a great brute of a Clydesdale. There was no saddle, so it was just as well that I had a firm backside. Most mornings the horse was pretty frisky and when he was like that, he took no end of catching. I tried everything: I even kept the bastard tied up one night, which was a good idea as far as I was concerned but the boss found out and gave me a swift kick up the arse for being lazy. Anyway, I would bring in the cows, yelling like a maniac into the cold morning air. Then the boss and I, and another fellow called Arnie, would milk them by hand. The milk was then loaded onto a horse-drawn milk cart and I'd have to help deliver it to the customers in Somerset Dam. When I returned from the milk delivery it was my job to sweep the bails, wash the milk cans and feed the horse. Then I would be given my breakfast out on the woodheap. Breakfast was usually leftovers from the previous night's meal.

Arnie was an illiterate Englishman who later got into some sort of strife: apparently he was a latent homosexual. I was really too young to understand what that was all about but, on reflection, I'm sure glad we slept in different buildings.

After about four months of this slavery I decided to tell the boss to stuff his cows, his horse and his milk run and headed back to the bush.

Old Tom Doyle was pleased to see me back. He wasn't feeling too well when I arrived, and asked me to give him a hand to yoke up his bullock team. The weather was threatening, so the pine logs lying up in the scrub had to be got out: first because they would turn green if they got wet; and second because there'd be no hope of getting the team up there once it started to rain. But old Tom was really crook.

'Why don't you go and have a lie down,' I urged him. 'Let me take the bastards up. I can snig those logs out.' He chewed on his filthy old pipe for a few moments and eyed me.

'Go on then, Bill,' he said. 'See what you can do. The timber truck is coming out from Esk today and he'll have to have a load.'

Well, I drove those bullocks into the scrub, plying my whip energetically, and had no difficulty in snigging out a couple of truckloads of logs. The wonga pigeons took off at the whip's first thunderous crack. If they could have held a conversation I feel sure they would have been saying, 'Look out! Mad Bill is back again!' Those cunning bullocks never did a harder day's work in their lives. Old Tom could swear, but I think I taught them a few new words. I believe that was the day I became a man.

A couple of weeks later, when Tom was feeling better, he split the team and gave me my own team of twelve bullocks. Tom's team continued to be uncooperative but mine worked with utmost alacrity, thanks to my thirty-foot whip.

Being isolated in the bush, we depended almost entirely on the timber truck to bring us our provisions, the most important of which were flour, corned brisket and tobacco. We rarely ran out of tea because we bought it by the seven-pound tin. You had to develop a strong stomach out in the bush to survive indefinitely on damper and cold, greasy corned brisket. I know it's somewhat romantic these days to dine on bush damper and syrup but when that's *all* you have, it can take a lot of hard swallowing at times.

For relaxation — and a change of tucker — during the weekend, I would take my 16-gauge shotgun and, with Ginger, my faithful turkey-dog, at my heels, walk for miles up and down those scrubby mountain ranges shooting scrub turkeys, wonga or flock pigeons. The dog would disappear for half an hour or so and then I'd hear him in the distance, barking like some crazed thing. He'd have treed a turkey. I would pelt off through the scrub like something equally crazed, falling over logs, getting jagged by thorny wild-plum vines (known in the bush as 'wait-a-whiles') and burnt by lawyer-cane vines. I always had a cartridge in the breech of my shotgun and how I managed not to blow my head off I'll never know! When I reached the now-frantic dog, sure enough, up in the highest branch of a tree would be squatting a plump turkey; up with the shotgun, and Blam! As the turkey hit the ground the dog would be upon it, and it took a lot of pulling to get him to release the still-fluttering bird from his slavering mouth.

Wonga pigeons were different. They were timid, and when you chased one up it would perch with its backside pointing towards you, ready to take off at the slightest move. They were delicious to eat, their flesh being soft and snow-white. Wonga pigeon soup was indeed a luxury in the bush. Flock pigeons were easy to shoot: they were so greedy that they took no notice of an approaching hunter as they fed off the figs of the huge Moreton Bay fig trees. One shot could bring down seven or more. They were not all that good to eat, but they sure beat cold, stale corned brisket.

After about two years in the solitude of the dense Queensland bush, which in this area was almost tropical jungle, I became a bit tired of it all. It was probably because I had no kids of my age to mix with. Tom Doyle had some sons, but they were much older than me. I was now thirteen years of age and, being a healthy, robust young man, I was beginning to feel a strong interest in the opposite sex. I suppose that was only natural, as were the occasional masturbation sessions behind a big tree up in the silence and privacy of the whispering bush.

One day I had had a gutful of privations of the wilderness, so I decided to jump on the timber truck and go to Toogoolawah to visit my stepfather's parents. Oh, dear: what a terrible scene *that* was. My mother pleaded with me not to leave home, telling me of all the terrible things that could befall me in the town. Of course, I listened to her, but I remained adamant. The call of nature was too great: I was determined to find out about life and I had to start somewhere.

I was still only a kid and, because of my enforced lack of schooling, unable to read anything except three or four-letter words.

But Mum eventually became resigned to the fact that I was off to visit that wide, mysterious world out there and after a while, instead of trying to frighten me out of it, she began giving me advice, not that she was a worldly woman.

'Stay away from the police,' she impressed upon me. 'Don't you pinch anything. You stay home at night.' And then, out it came: 'You keep away from those girls, Billy,' she warned. 'They'll only get you into trouble.'

Dear old Mum. I smiled as I thought, '*Who* is going to get *whom* into trouble?' Some of Tom Doyle's kids had oiled me up about what to do with sheilas. Whacko!

After a couple of weeks in Toogoolawah with my German stepgrandparents, or whatever they were, I somehow managed to scrounge the sixpence I needed to get into the pictures. There I met Dorothy, an old school friend; she was my age and we got along together. When the pictures came out we walked around for a while and ended up on the steps of the Toogoolawah Post Office. We mucked about a bit: she was just as willing and anxious as I was to discover the secrets of life and, I suspect, just as ignorant about such matters. Anyway, in the excitement of the moment I completely forgot my mother's words of warning and started to run my hand up her leg, past the knee. This is what the Doyle boys had told me was the correct procedure, and in any case, it seemed the natural thing to do. She didn't object, and eventually my fingers came in contact with hair. This sort of took me by surprise because I had thought only boys had hair there. It suddenly dawned on me that I didn't have a clue what my next move was supposed to be — the Doyle boys hadn't been explicit enough! I panicked and fled, leaving the poor girl sitting bewildered on the post office steps.

I met Dorothy in the street the next day.

'Why did you run away?' she asked me.

'I got frightened,' I admitted, unashamedly. 'What was I suppose to do? Do you know?'

'I think so,' she answered shyly. 'I saw my mother and father doing it once. I think I could figure it out.'

We made a date to meet again that night and I was determined not to chicken out this time. I trembled at the thought of it: where was my mother now?

We met outside the fruit shop and must have walked for miles before we plucked up the courage to stop. Before us was an empty house. As it was fairly light in the full moon, we decided to go into the laundry.

'We've got to lie down,' she informed me. I looked down at the broken concrete floor.

'But it's all wet and rough down there,' I complained.

'We could do it standing up,' she suggested. Standing up? My mind boggled at the impossibility of it all.

'How?' I sought her guidance.

'I dunno,' she replied. 'But it's possible. I've heard people talk about it. It's called a "knee-trembler". '

Well, I thought, if she has heard people talking about it, it must be possible; she's the experienced one. It wasn't all that dark, even inside the laundry, but we had no inhibitions about dropping our pants. She was up against something firm and I pressed myself against her. It felt pleasurable but I didn't have a clue what I was doing or what I was supposed to do next. All I knew was that I was supposed to do *something*. Dark thoughts flashed across my mind: You wait till I see those rotten Doyle boys again!

As I pressed myself harder against her, there was a resounding crash. Well, you never saw two people jump back into their pants so quickly in your life! Apparently Dorothy had been leaning up against a wooden clothes trolley and our combined weight had caused it to collapse. That fearful noise, in the dead of the night, scared the hell out of both of us and we took off at a rapid rate. Even though we were almost dying with fright, we were both laughing so much we had to stop and sit down on the soft, cool grass.

When we could laugh no longer we lay on the grass and hugged each other, overcome by each other's innocence. Somehow everything went right this time and Dorothy, dear, sensuous little girl, gave me the first and most memorable sex lesson of my life, and one of the most beautiful memories I have of growing up.

Chapter 2

A few weeks later my step-grandparents told me of a good job they had found for me. Actually, I don't think they had my interests at heart — I guess I'd begun to wear out my welcome. The 'good job' was on another dairy farm, in the Kilcoy District. The owner was another German, called 'Retchleg', or something like that.

Well, I spent the next few months milking cows, pulling corn, feeding pigs and trying to get on to his luscious fifteen-year-old daughter who had legs that would have made Betty Grable envious. The mental images I conjured up of her and me down in the corn patch are better imagined than described. But I had no hope with her: she had some idiot from a neighbouring farm in tow. If only I could have taught her the lessons Dorothy had taught me. I was quite willing to pass on all my knowledge to her. Oh, well, back to Mrs Palmer and her five daughters!

The boss was a typical high-bred Hun who didn't swear, was an avid churchgoer and said grace before meals; and he didn't like to see me smoking. I hated the fat, conceited bastard. He nagged me and threatened to kick my arse, but if he'd touched me I would have flattened him with a pitchfork. I got tired of his moralistic attitudes. So off I went, back to my beloved bush, much to Mum's delight and relief. I'm sure she had expected me to have a woman and half a dozen kids in tow by now. She wanted to know where I had been and what I had been doing, but thankfully she didn't press me too much about what I had been doing in my spare time.

I went back to bullock driving and timber cutting. My old shotgun had become a bit rusty and my faithful turkey-dog Ginger, who had led me on so many mad scrambles through the bush, had caught a scrub tick and was becoming paralysed. I gave him a bush remedy of gunpowder and fat but he was too far gone and I had to destroy him. It almost broke my heart. It takes either a courageous man or a brutal man to point a gun at the head of his faithful dog and pull the trigger. In truth, I am neither; I simply did what had to be done. I think that was the day I questioned the existence of God in earnest. I still question it today, but I leave my options open, just in case.

Although I had been away only about two years, Mum looked a lot older. She had had a rough, tough life. Being part Aboriginal, she had been taken away from her mother while young and placed in a mission. From there, she went into the Sir Leslie Wilson Home for Girls, in Brisbane. At sixteen she was turfed out into the world knowing even less than I did at her age. By the age of seventeen, she had become pregnant with me and was left to cope on her own. I never knew my father, and he should be grateful for that: he'd had his pleasures and then, like a mongrel dog, had slunk away. Now, here Mum was, cooking over an open fire. She boiled the potatoes and pumpkin in six-pound powdered milk tins and boiled the washing in four-gallon kerosene tins. Her husband, my stepfather, used to knock her about a bit until one day I hit him on the shin with the back of my axe. It curbed him a bit. There was nothing he could do about it because I was more than a match for him. I was just as rough and tough as he was but I was younger and, thanks to the hard work I had done, as powerful as a working bullock. He was a real rifle fanatic and had several rifles in the camp. He threatened Mum with a rifle one day so I walked into Somerset Dam, about fifteen miles away, and dobbed him in to the police sergeant. Sergeant Lucy drove me back to the camp and confronted my stepfather, the butt of a revolver obvious as it protruded warningly out of his side pocket.

'You got some firearms here?' he asked my stepfather.

'No, I got no bloody guns here,' he replied.

'Lyin' bastard,' I said to him. I turned to Sergeant Lucy. 'They're hanging from the ridgepole in the tent.'

The old man gave me a withering look and I returned it with one of contempt. Yes, he did Mum a favour when he died.

A year or so after my return, my stepfather died up in the bush from a brain haemorrhage. Mum collected his worker's compensation, about two thousand pounds, which was the only thing of value she ever got from him; even then, he had to die to be of any use to her.

About a week after his death Mum packed her belongings into tea-chests and moved to Brisbane, where she took a flat. I told her I would follow in a few days' time. It was now about eighteen months since I had left Toogoolawah, and I was keen to go there to see Dorothy again. But when I saw her standing in front of Flaska the Greek's cafe, she looked different; her stomach wasn't as streamlined and comely as I'd remembered it.

Chapter Two

I hitched a ride to Brisbane and stayed with Mum for a few weeks. I had to sponge off her because I was broke, as usual. Then I saw an advertisement in the *Courier-Mail* for a dairy hand. It was the only job in the city that I was capable of doing, so I applied for it and my application was successful. The name of the dairy was Glendalough, in the Brisbane suburb of Wilston. (There is no sign of the dairy now, of course; the entire area is covered with housing estates.) This job was similar to the first one I had: milking cows and delivering milk.

There was another bloke, about twenty-five years of age, working at the dairy, who had the mistaken idea that I was just a dumb kid from the bush. He needled me daily until I finally jacked up and gave him the full benefit of my bullock-driving vernacular. He took exception to this and challenged me to a fight. Apparently he did a bit of boxing around the ridges, and his friends told me that my days were numbered.

They made a boxing ring in the barn by placing bales of straw and bags of chaff to form a square. I had never had a real grown-up fight in my life, only those skirmishes down behind the school sports pavilion in Toogoolawah when the kids would chide me about being a nigger. But that was only kid stuff; this coming fight was the real thing: boxing gloves, resin boxes, the lot. The fight was fairly well advertised among my opponent's mates and they turned up in droves to watch the slaughter — my slaughter!

Well, the fight duly got under way and I found that boxing came naturally to me. There was blood everywhere: *his* blood. He ended up an absolute pulp. I really felt sorry for him because I had broken his jaw in three places and his nose was a bloody mess. I got cocky then and asked his mates if any of them wanted to have a go. No way — it was instant fame.

It was rather sad to see my erstwhile opponent wired up for the next several weeks. A fight had been the last thing I wanted, but a bloke can only cop so much. I was treated with respect, if not awe, after the fight.

I was still working at Glendalough dairy on 13 May 1943, the day I turned sixteen. That day I caught a tram at the Grange terminus and went in to the enlistment office at Petrie Bight. Of course, I had to put my age up to eighteen which was the legal enlistment age, but I was a hefty bloke and had no difficulty in convincing the enlistment officer that I was indeed eighteen, and I was readily accepted. After a few short, perfunctory tests and examinations I was in.

By now I could read reasonably well. I had got tired of missing out on the obvious enjoyment of reading things other than Mandrake comics, which I could scarcely understand, anyway. So I pinched a dictionary and a Foulshams Letter Writer and after much thumbing of the pages began to understand what it was all about. I was still not so hot on writing though. Actually, I still find it difficult to sit down and write a letter in longhand. But I get by.

So here I was, no longer a second-class citizen, but a member of the Royal Australian Air Force, and Aircraftsman First Class — or AC1, as we were called. The enlistment officer spruiked to all who would listen that here was a young man who was prepared to die for king and country. Bullshit! I wasn't *that* keen. But the uniforms were warm and had no 'spuds' in them and I was issued with a pair of shoes and a pair of boots, the very first footwear I had ever put on my feet in my life.

When I first spoke with the enlistment officer, I had told him I wanted to be an air gunner.

'Have you had any experience with guns?' he asked me, as he threw out his pugnacious jaw. I told him I had, but I don't think my answer mattered too much. They were desperate for machine-gunners, or so I was told.

I flew through my 'rookies' (basic training) and enjoyed every minute of it. We had to roll out of bed at 6 am, which was no problem because, unlike many of my fellow AC1s, I had been conditioned to early rising by my past life on dairy farms. I took to the RAAF lifestyle like a duck to water, leaving most of the other trainees for dead as far as stamina and keenness were concerned. Part of our training consisted of negotiating obstacle courses. I was through them almost before the others had thought about it. And why not? — I was tough, wiry and mountain bred, like the horses from Snowy River. I remember one time during our training when the training officer dropped us miles out in scrubby outback country and set us the difficult task of finding our own way back. Back at the camp, the officer was just about to sit down with a mug of tea when I came up behind him, and spoke to him. Well, you would have thought a black snake had bitten him. Tea flew everywhere. He was quite red in the face as he turned to me.

'Christ!' he expostulated. 'Didn't you go out with the others?'

'Yes, sir,' I replied, nervously.

'Well,' he demanded, 'how the bloody hell did you get back here? I only dropped you off an hour ago.'

'I ran through the bush and followed the creek, sir.' He took up what remained of his tea.

'Where are the others?' he enquired.

'Buggered if I know, sir.' He was clearly impressed with my efforts in not only finding my way back, but in returning so quickly. He knew I hadn't got a lift because it was all bush country and out of bounds to other vehicles. So pleased was he that he proffered me a mug of his tea. It was unheard of for an officer to fraternise with a lowly enlisted man in this manner, but he was a friendly, good-natured bloke — I think he must have been bush bred, too. Anyway my years of running up mountains, swinging an axe and flogging bullocks were beginning to pay off.

When my rookie training was completed I was posted to Number 1 Bombing and Gunnery School at Evans Head — 'No. 1 BAGS', we called it. Evans Head were using old Fairey Battles as training aircraft. They were equipped with twin-barrel Vickers machine-guns placed in the rear cockpit. The idea was to sit in the cockpit and, when a few miles out to sea, shoot at a drogue target being towed by another Fairey Battle. The trouble was that, since the windsock was made of cloth, there was no way of telling if you had hit it or not. Nevertheless, I was doing really well and was thoroughly enjoying myself, until one day when I fired an extra long burst. Unfortunately I hadn't noticed that the port wing of our aircraft was across my line of fire and before I knew it, a row of jagged holes had appeared along its length. The pilot panicked and did a sickening 'split-arse' turn to starboard, but it was too late: my aim had been deadly. We got back to Base and landed safely, but the tirade I received from both the pilot and my commanding officer rivalled anything I could have done with my bullock-driving vocabulary. I was hauled before a group of officers who held an enquiry into the incident and I was 'grounded'. What a disgrace: fancy almost shooting your own aircraft down! I copped a lot of good-natured chiacking from my mates over it and the only response I could make was to give a stupid grin.

I forget how long they grounded me for, but it was too long for me. I wasn't prepared to sit around and miss out on the excitement of air force life. So I told them to shove their Fairey Battles and their Vickers machine-guns, in polite terms, of course, and asked to be remustered.

I looked up the various musterings available and the one which took my fancy was 'guard'. To become a guard it was necessary to do an unarmed combat course, lasting about three months, at Shepparton RAAF Base, in Victoria. This appealed to my sense of adventure, and the rough and tumble of the training would suit me as I was simply bursting for physical activity. Besides the unarmed combat, there was also a course on weaponry. What fun! I was still only sixteen but I had a mature mind and body, and I was champing at the bit.

The training was all I had hoped it would be. It was hard, bone-breaking work, but it was fun too. I enjoyed the mock battles with the other blokes, who were all pretty tough. You could let yourself go and half kill each other; we were even encouraged to do this, but we enjoyed every minute of it. At the completion of the course came the 'passing out', and I was promoted to leading aircraftsman. It sounded impressive but it still was only the equivalent of a lance corporal in the army. I was issued with two blue linen propellers, which were to be sewn onto the sleeves of my uniform. I made sure that, as I walked, my arms were held a bit more forward than usual. I wanted everybody to notice those propellers. Such is the vanity of youth.

I was given two weeks' leave and issued with a rail pass. At Evans Head railway station the Railway Transport Officer (RTO) put me on the right train for Brisbane: I was off to visit my mother. When she saw me, resplendent in my blue dress uniform, she began to cry. She wept because she was pleased to see me, her only child, but also, I fancy, because she had conjured up visions of me lying dead on some far-distant battlefield. I brought a smile back to her face by telling her that it would take a little longer for me to win the war. Then I made the smile a little more permanent by telling her that the war would be over long before I was ready to be sent away as gun fodder: I told her I had heard high-ranking officers say so but to keep it a secret because I wasn't supposed to hear them. This appeared to calm her down somewhat, but I think she secretly felt that I was a bit of a bullshit artist!

Since coming to Brisbane she had met a Scotsman called David, a drunken sod if ever there was one. But she had been lonely and she liked him and he seemed to be doing the right thing by her, so I accepted the situation. They were married later and he turned out to be an adequate provider and treated Mum all right regardless of his mostly inebriated condition. He went to the pub with his mates every day after work and drank himself stupid. Ten days later I said goodbye to my tearful mother and boarded another troop train and headed back to Shepparton. In three days' time I would be due back at the Base.

When I arrived back I got a bit of a shock. Lorna, an English girl with whom I had become friendly — she was a member of the Women's Royal Australian Air Force (WRAAF) — told me she was pregnant. Christ! Mum had warned me that this could happen. But I hadn't heeded Mum's advice during my mating sessions down behind the butter factory. Now I recalled how cold it had been in the dead of night behind that butter factory, lying on my air force-issue overcoat. How I had shivered! But my shivering had been overcome by the orgastic delights we shared.

Of course, I had no option but to do the right thing and marry the girl. I shuddered at what my mother would say. I had to tell her because at sixteen I was still a minor and I had to have her written consent to marry. I wrote to her and told her all the details. Well, most of them, anyway. I sucked up to her a bit by telling her how great it would be for her to have a daughter in the family. She never commented on this remark, but I'd like to have seen her face when she read my scribbled letter. Surprisingly, she didn't crack up much at all except for the well-deserved 'I told you so'.

We were married in Scots Church, in Melbourne. We were granted compassionate leave for a honeymoon, which seemed silly because, since I had met her, life had been one big honeymoon! She was eventually discharged from the WRAAF and, during another leave, I brought her up to Brisbane to meet my mother. They got on all right but I think Mum secretly resented the fact that Lorna had taken her little boy away from her and taught him nasty tricks. That's the trouble with being an only child: mothers seem to think they never grow up, while other people think they're spoilt.

Things didn't go too well for me during the months that followed. I developed epilepsy and towards the end of 1944 was boarded out of the Service on medical grounds. So there I was, not yet eighteen years of age but with a wife, and soon a child, to look after. So I went back to the only work I knew; I went back to the bush. Several months later our beautiful baby girl was born. We called her Joy Lorraine.

I took a job at Wyanga Creek, at the back of Somerset Dam, clearing paddocks of lantana and spotted gum trees. It was hard work. We lived in a tent and Lorna, a city-bred girl, loved every minute of bush life. Life in the bush wasn't easy for her, but she was a spirited girl and tried to help me in my work. But I was always whingeing at her because she would hit into the dirt and make my axe blunt. I would then have to spend hours grinding the face of it to regain its keenness. It would be half a day wasted.

To watch her cook in the bush was a scream. She had no idea about bush tucker or how to prepare it, with the result that we practically lived on tinned meat and tinned fish. But we got on well and had a lot of fun. I will never forget the day we were cuddling up in the shade of a huge she-oak tree and somehow lost control of ourselves. We were miles out in the bush with nobody around, so we began to do what came naturally. We were in a complete state of euphoria when a man rode past on horseback. Of course, we were galvanised into instant evasive action. I have no idea what the interloper thought but he just rode on past. It is possible he didn't even notice us: perhaps the hypnotic swaying of his horse had put him to sleep. Who knows? Lorna and I laughed for weeks about the incident. As Lorna remarked, stolen fruit is the sweetest.

The rains came and chased us out of the bush. A tent is no place to live in when the seasonal storms begin, especially with a young child. We moved into the township of Esk where I got a job cutting down trees and then chopping their trunks into six-foot lengths. They would be picked up later, tossed onto a truck, and taken into Esk to be cut into stove lengths with a circular saw. It was gut-busting work. We boarded at one of the local pubs; it was dry, cool and comfortable. Lorna didn't have to cook and there was no washing dishes, sweeping floors or making beds. Lorna had a ball while we stayed at that pub.

The time had come, as I knew it must, when Lorna wanted to go to see her mother. She lived in Adelaide, in the suburb of Swansea. We called in to visit my mother on the way through, then boarded a train at South Brisbane station. Eons later, it seemed to me, we pulled into Adelaide. Lorna's mother was not at all like my mother. She was a snooty, stuck-up woman who, when she looked at me, appeared to be looking down her long, angular nose. How I loathed her superior attitude. When she discovered from Lorna that I was of Aboriginal descent she went off her brain chastising her for 'getting mixed up with a dirty blackfellow'. Funnily enough, since I had left school I had lost track of the fact that I was 'different'. If I keep out of the sun for long enough I can easily pass for a white person with a healthy suntan, except for my bulbous nose.

Lorna had given birth to another baby, a girl, prior to our coming to Adelaide, and my mother-in-law fussed over the baby and resented my having anything to do with her. She was an overbearing woman and, perhaps because of this, Lorna seemed to take sides with her against me. She had a brother, a rather effeminate young man, and he joined in the conspiracy. This was having quite some effect on the relationship between us, which Lorna was loath to discuss with me. I suggested that we return to Queensland but she would have none of it. We stayed four months, gradually growing further apart; we didn't seem to have things in common any more. The beautiful camaraderie which we had once enjoyed faded to a whisper, until one day, when

I returned from a shopping expedition, I discovered her romping on the bed with a guide from the local automobile club. I became temporarily deranged, and left them both lying on the bedroom floor, each a broken, bloody mess. I felt shame for what I had done, and experienced an overwhelming hatred of myself. I was heartbroken.

I caught a train back to Queensland that night and I never saw Lorna or the kids again. I tried desperately to locate them a month or so later but they were nowhere to be found, and her mother would give me no help. I advertised in the papers for months without response. I found out, years later, that Lorna had changed her name to his by deed poll. No wonder I was unable to find them. It took a while but I put the memory behind me. However, I will never forgive her mother for what she did.

Chapter 3

After receiving solace from various kind-hearted, understanding women who were liberal with their charms, I began to feel my old self again. I have discovered in life that there is nothing like a woman to break a man but, by golly, there is nothing like a woman to get the old tail standing upright again either.

I paid a long visit to Mum and David in Brisbane, and then decided that I wanted to see a bit more of Australia. I had very little money and the only economical way to go was by hitch-hiking. Then I met Johnny, an old mate of mine who had the same desire. We got a bit of a swag together and off we went. We had no trouble in getting rides in those days — this was the 1950s — and we took jobs along the way to pay for our few needs. I think Johnny must have been a bit of a blackfellow, too; he would eat anything and sleep anywhere. We chipped burrs from creek banks, cut sugarcane in New South Wales, fertilised bananas, and did anything else that came along. There was plenty of work, but whether we took it or not depended on the state of our stomachs. If we were hungry, we worked; if we were flush, we lived the good life. We stayed together for about six months, but apparently Johnny had done something shady in the past and one day a detective stopped his police car and called him over. From what I could glean from the detective's conversation, Johnny's crime had been to nick a radio somewhere along the line. The police arrested him on the spot, and before I knew it they had put him in the slammer. This was obviously no place for me, so I hotfooted it back to Brisbane just as fast as I could.

I was drinking tea and idly looking through the Positions Vacant columns of the *Courier-Mail* one day when I spotted a job I thought I might like: feeding and looking after chooks on an egg farm. I applied for and got the job; the chook farm was at Tarragindi, then regarded as a rather distant suburb of Brisbane.

Also working there was Lillian, a slip of a girl about fifteen years old. I was twenty-three. She was quite a comely wench. She showed me what to do around the place and, both being naturally playful people, we often had egg fights in the fowl houses with frantic chooks flying and shitting all over the place, their squawking drowned out by the squeals of our mischievous felicity. We became friendly, then quite friendly, then infatuated. We were married on her sixteenth birthday. We took a job as a married couple on a dairy farm up at Mt Mee, a name without a township. The nearest township was a place called Dayboro. It had a butter factory too!

After a month or so Vic Britten, the owner, told us he would put us on half shares. This sounded good, so we accepted the offer. But once we had agreed to go half shares in the dairy with him, he used to disappear at milking times. He would be down in the barn pulling some old tractor to pieces or trying to get some ancient plough to work. I got jack of this, so I lined him up one day down at the barn.

'Listen,' I said to him, 'fuck you for a joke! If you want half the profits from the cows, you do half the work.'

My words pulled him into gear a bit but he was still lazy. He began picking on my wife, almost reducing her to tears on several occasions.

'Now, look here,' I said, at last, 'if you don't get off her back I'll bend this shovel over your pinhead.'

His eyes opened wide with surprise: he hadn't expected me to be quite so forceful or threatening. But he got the message and kept his tongue to himself; he sulked for days. We were still friendly enough, I suppose. After all, to make this farm pay, we had to work together. He knew it and I knew it.

Actually, there was no way in the world that farm was going to make us a fortune. We could only afford bread-and-butter items. We had plenty of meat though; when we were running short all we had to do was slaughter a calf or yearling or even a nice plump pig.

We were in the grip of a drought and, as it progressed, things on the farm became much worse. We barely had enough feed for the cows during the winter months, which I put down to Vic's bad management the previous year. He had planted no cow cane or sorghum, or anything else that could be turned into chaff. Cows began to die from lack of calcium. Many nights I sat up, injecting calcium into them every hour or so. This overcame their calcium deficiency but caused them to become soporific, with the result that they couldn't eat. Eventually Vic and I had to take an outside job, chipping banana patches, to keep the farm going. This didn't suit me at all. I was buggered if I was going to slave my guts out in order to feed bloody cows! So Vic and I had a talk and he ended up borrowing 100 pounds from his bank, which he gave to me. The next day Lillian and I hitched a ride in the cream truck into Dayboro. From there we went to Zillmere, where Lillian's parents, Eric and Biddy, lived in a Housing Commission house. We stayed with them for a good while, during which time Lillian gave birth to our first child, a son. We named him Eric (after Lillian's father) William (after me) but usually called him 'Rick'.

Biddy was pretty good as mothers-in-law go — nothing like Lorna's mother back in Adelaide. Eric was a real good bloke, too. He was partly deaf so he had got himself one of these hearing devices. He stuck the earpiece in his ear, of course, and rammed the bulky box-like container which held the batteries and the guts of the device down the front of his shirt. He always amused me when he answered the phone: he would turn the receiver upside down, place the earpiece hard up to his stomach, and then shout into the mouthpiece. He had half the index finger missing from his left hand and used to frighten old ladies on the trams by placing the butt of the finger onto his nostril, giving the appearance that he had the entire finger shoved up his nose. He's still a funny bugger, old Eric; a nicer bloke you couldn't wish to meet. Biddy, on the other hand, was a bit of a whinger and I think she had every reason to be. The poor unfortunate woman suffered with a huge ulcer on her leg that just wouldn't heal. She limped around for years on that leg, doing all the housework. The amount of washing alone would have done credit to a Chinese laundry. She had seven kids; no wonder her back was stooped.

Work was becoming scarce, and I was forced to go on the dole a few months before our second child was born. We called her Kathryn Lynette. We stayed with Eric and Biddy for a long time, occasionally having our differences, but in the main we all got on well together.

When Rick was about three years old, we took a flat in Fortitude Valley which, I suppose, could be classed as part of the City of Brisbane. I took a job as a metal polisher but I didn't last long there. The foreman was the biggest crawler, and liar, I have ever known. Finally, four of us, being unable to take his disgraceful behaviour any longer, simply walked up to the boss, and told him we were leaving and to make up our pays. Of course, we each lost a day's pay in lieu of notice, but it was worth it: our self-respect and our dignity remained intact.

In any case, I was yearning once more for the bush.

Lillian liked the bush, too — mainly, I suspect, because there was no housework to do. I don't mean that unkindly: housework must have been a pain, particularly with an untidy bloke like me around.

So, back to the bush we went, where we were later to have our third child. I took on a job timber-felling. Lillian tried to assist me in my work but the tools were far too heavy for her. She wasn't a big girl and when she slung a bag of steel wedges over her back she buckled at the knees. So she stuck to boiling the billy and making countless mugs of tea.

A year or so later I read somewhere that unimproved land was selling cheap down around Beenleigh. Lillian was pregnant again, so we gave the bush away and bought eight acres south of Slack's Creek, about ten miles south of Brisbane. I secured a job at a nearby pottery and then got big ideas about building a house. I built a rough shack to start with; it served the purpose but water was a constant problem. So I built a wall across an adjoining creek. This, of course, was quite illegal, but nobody said anything and it solved our water problem. The block was heavily wooded so I had to clear an area upon which to build my house. Unfortunately the entire eight acres were covered with black wattle trees and spotted gum, none of which was suitable as mill timber; all of that had been scrounged out long ago. I wasn't enchanted with the prospect of digging bloody great holes around the trunks of trees in order to get them out, so I hit upon a sure-fire plan: I would blast them out! I was reasonably familiar with explosives as we had used it in the bush to blast a road through the scrub for the timber truck.

I purchased some gelignite, detonator caps and miles of fuse. I strapped three or four plugs of the gelignite around the trunk of the first tree, inserted the cap, and lit the fuse. Boy! Did that tree lift! It came crashing down in a splintered mess. And so it went on. As far as clearing my land was concerned, the hard work was over; only the excitement of my frenzied retreat after I lit the fuses and watching the trees erupt into matchsticks remained. Some of my neighbours — all battlers and just as broke as I was — came around to my block to watch the fun. After each blast and when the sticks and stones had all hurtled back down from the sky, they would emerge from behind various points of cover, shaking with anticipation of the next furious blast.

I had now been working at the pottery for about six months and knew the job backwards. I suggested to the boss that he send pottery to country places like Mt Isa and Rockhampton. He said it was not a good idea so I finished up at the pottery, sold my land, and went up to Townsville where I started my own pottery business (and we had our fifth, and last, child). There was a wrought-iron craze on at the time so I made wrought-iron furniture too. Finding I couldn't handle all the work, I invited a friend to come up and work on a half-share basis. I found out, too late, that he was a sneaky little bastard, and pretty soon my firm had gone broke.

Chapter Three 23

Truly, some people just never learn!

Back in Brisbane, I discovered that as an ex-serviceman I was entitled to a War Service home. I lost no time in buying a block of land at Petrie, north of Brisbane, and before long had a nice shiny new house built on it. We had it painted bright yellow, Lillian's favourite colour. I bought furniture, on time payment, and settled down, just as a family man ought to.

I worked at a brickworks at Strathpine for three years, which entitled me to join their superannuation scheme. But on the very day I completed my three years I was sacked along with three other employees who had started there with me. Rotten bastards!

I wasn't out of work for long, however: a week later I got a job as a builder's labourer, working on the new Festival Hall, in Albert Street, Brisbane. I was teamed up with an arrogant young German fellow; between us we placed and tied just about all the reinforcing steel throughout the building. The job was just about complete when the contractor, Eddie Taylor, went broke. Out of work again — talk about unlucky!

Chapter 4

At about the time I left my Festival Hall job, I was starting to become more aware of the 'Aboriginal problem' in Queensland. I can't remember exactly what was the catalyst for my involvement. It was probably a combination of many things. I remember particularly, though, the report of a young black girl's experiences when she reported having been raped by a white man at Mt Gravatt. At the police station a police officer accused her of having been 'fucked' before, and of having 'enjoyed it' (that is, the rape). When she replied, 'Yes, I've been fucked before, but I've just been raped. What are you going to do about it?', she was charged with using insulting language to the police, and ended up in prison. No action was ever taken against the rapist. On another occasion, I was present when three young Aboriginal boys were thrown out of a near-Brisbane swimming pool, with the order, 'Hey you blackfellas, get the hell out of here. You know you bastards aren't allowed in here!' (For more details on these incidents see *This is Palm Island*.)

In the late 1960s I began going to blacks' meetings to learn more about the injustices Queensland's Aborigines were suffering under the State Government, and eventually became a member of the original Brisbane Aboriginal and Islanders Council, which elected as its executive Brisbane's first Aboriginal Tribal Council. The council was formed in 1969 to fight for a say in policy making on matters concerning Aborigines and Islanders. Blacks were sick and tired of police victimisation and violence, and the racism within the police force. At our meetings, held several times each month, we discussed the latest outrages and made plans as to what action we should take. Of course, there was precious little we could do about it: if we approached the police, all we could expect was a thumping, or some trumped-up charge. No one listened to blackfellows in those days. I was also involved in the Aboriginal Legal Service, where a major concern was the ease with which the police had access to confidential legal files. The Tribal Council organised street marches, and letters of protest to the Police Commissioner, the Director of Aboriginal Affairs and the Premier, but nothing did any good; all we got was bad press. But I think just to meet and talk about it helped us deal with our frustrations. At least we were among others who understood our problems, and we were able to console one another.

Our council was plagued by a bunch of fanatics who called themselves the 'Young Communist League'. They feigned allegiance to the Aboriginal cause, but, in my opinion, they were interested only in their own agenda. Their intrusion did nothing for our image; they raved and ranted, and walked around waving stupid red flags, telling people how badly done by Aborigines were. This only served to inflame the average man in the street, to whom communism was a scourge on society. They introduced us to the Waterside Workers Federation, telling us that, as a powerful union, they could help us in our fight for self-determination. So we attended their meetings and they passed motion after motion, but with no result.

We weren't a political organisation; politics meant nothing to us. We simply wanted the right to get a job, rent a flat or house, enter a bar if we wanted to, obtain effective health care, have our kids accepted in schools, and have the police stop harassing us.

I also became a member of the Born Free Club, a club which, according to its 1972 constitution, aimed to listen to Aborigines' and Islanders' problems; take a stand on issues; smash discrimination against the blacks, particularly in hotels; and discuss with parents their children's problems at school. We tried to give a bit of a helping hand to Aborigines, including a place for them to sleep. We cleaned up the basement of an old hotel on the corner of Melbourne and Stanley Streets, in South Brisbane, and furnished it with beds and mattresses — old, but usable — that we were given by a church organisation. When it rained, the entire floor went under about eight inches of water. We kept it going with our own money, and donations from sympathetic white people, most of whom had no more to spare than we did.

We had a few stoushes there, too. Occasionally a group of Aborigines from nearby areas would come to the city, intent on fighting and brawling with their city counterparts; one night things became so bad that Don Davidson and I tore palings from a nearby fence and whaled into the fray, finally putting the interlopers to rout. I believe some of them were escorted to the city watch-house by police, who were never far away. Why they wanted to fight I really don't know; perhaps it was tribal oriented, the animosity of which extended back for hundreds of years.

During one of the Born Free Club's meetings it was decided that one of our group should attend a coming conference of the Federal

Council for the Advancement of Aboriginals and Torres Strait Islanders (FCAATSI), which was to be held in Townsville. It was put to a vote and I was elected to be the club's representative. This was to be probably the most fateful event of my life: it was at this meeting that I was invited to visit Palm Island for the first time, and it was as a consequence of this visit that I began my writing career.

We managed to scrape enough money together for the fare, and off I went. When you attend an Aboriginal meeting, anything can happen, and usually does; so you've got to be alert and ready for anything. But this meeting turned out to be a timid affair. There were a few militant blacks, but they were still inexperienced in political matters.

It was at this meeting that I met Iris Clay. She was about four feet eight inches tall, and weighed not much over seven stone. Seeing her in action was quite an experience. She attacked the Federal Department of Aboriginal Affairs, condemning them for their poor efforts regarding black rights, and told the Queensland Department of Aboriginal and Islanders Affairs just what she thought about the Director, Queensland's *Aborigines Act*, and the Palm Island Reserve manager. She also took on the representative of the Aboriginal Legal Service.

Iris was a very aware person who knew what it was all about. Anyone who crossed her, either at a meeting or out in the street, was asking for trouble. Her husband, Fred Clay, was the Chairman of the Palm Island Aboriginal Council.

Iris and I sat together at the Townsville meeting and we became friends, sympathetic to the same cause. I told her a bit about myself and what I was doing in Brisbane, and she invited me over to Palm Island for the weekend to meet Fred and to have a look at the place. Iris had an earlier appointment on the island, so it was arranged that I would board the light aircraft on the Saturday morning and fly to Palm Island where I would be met and taken to the Clays' home.

Palm Island is a small island twenty-odd miles off the east coast of north Queensland. The Queensland Government established a settlement there in 1918 when the inhabitants of the Hull River settlement, which was destroyed by a cyclone, were relocated to Palm Island. It later became a penal settlement, administered by the Queensland Government, and later an Aboriginal reserve. At the time I first visited it, about 1,200 people were living there.

Of course I had heard stories of life on the island, as well as vague references to happenings there in occasional news bulletins.

Usually these referred to some Aboriginal uprising against white authority, invariably because of conditions suffered by the island's black inhabitants, and the treatment meted out to them under the Queensland *Aborigines Act*. During the previous two days, I had heard a lot more. Now I was going to the island to find out for myself.

This is how I described my first impressions of Palm Island in another book (*This is Palm Island*):

> I looked out through my window and saw the most beautiful island I had ever seen. Palm Island was studded with coconut and mango trees. Almost all of the island was covered in brilliant green foliage. The waves were breaking gently over the pure white sands of the beach ... Shoals of fish were quite near the beach. Surely, even I, the worst fisherman in the world, would be able to catch a fish here ... The aircraft made a sudden turn and bank to starboard and there, dead ahead, lay a small landing field. On one side of the strip there was a dense forest and on the other a large swamp.
>
> A community bus took us from the airport to the Palm Island settlement, about three kilometres up the road. The road was the worst I have ever travelled on, with great wash-outs on one side, and a precipitous drop of about 150 metres on the other. Only the genius of Johnny Tarpaulin, the driver, got us there in one piece.
>
> I received a warm welcome from Fred Clay, who proved to be as dedicated to the black cause as Iris was, and fought for it just as hard. From the beginning, I saw evidence of how the Act affected all aspects of life on the island. I had actually got my first indication even before I boarded the plane. It was all right, I was told, for a white man to take alcohol onto the island, but a black man would be taken to court and charged for doing the same thing. But what I heard from Fred and Iris Clay made me determined to stay and find out more about life on the island, and do what I could to help.

Here are just a few of the restrictions imposed on the Aboriginal people of Palm Island:

> People who wanted to go swimming in the sea had first to parade before the manager of the reserve so that he could ascertain if, in his opinion, they were correctly dressed for such an occasion.
>
> If a person wanted (or needed) to go to the mainland, for whatever reason, a written permit had first to be given by the

manager. A similar permit had to be obtained by any Aborigine wanting to visit (or live on) Palm Island (Section 23, clause 1, subclause [a]).

Any person could be 'exiled' from the island for the 'well-being' of the Aboriginal community; so too could his or her children. There was no redress; there was nothing the people could do. If they kicked up a fuss they would be summarily put in prison — no charge, no formal arrest!

It was forbidden to utter words of protest or to criticise the manager or any other authority. If you did so, you could be 'removed from the reserve with as much force as is deemed necessary'.

Aborigines were not allowed to practise traditional dances or ceremonies except with the written permission of the manager. To do so was an infringement of the Act and the participants could be put into prison. (This is the most restrictive rule which, ultimately, led to the downfall of Aboriginal society: the denial to Aborigines of practising their own culture and customs. That particular clause (Section 21, clause 1) spelt doom to the Aboriginal race as it had been.)

Permission had to be gained from the manager of the reserve if you wanted to get married. If the manager did not agree to the marriage he refused permission (Section 19, clause [b]).

Alcohol was not permitted in the homes of blacks. It was issued only at the canteen, and rationed to four cans three times a week.

Blacks could live only in designated areas of the island.

Because the house Fred, as Chairman of the Tribal Council, was to live in had been damaged, and also because of Fred's high standing in the community, the Clays were living in a white area. But when he wanted to have alcohol there, the reserve manager simply took his map and shaded in the area representing Fred's yard, announcing that it was now a reserve. This was a typical example of how the rules could change to suit the convenience of the island's manager or the Director of the Department of Aboriginal Affairs.

Blacks on the island earned only a pittance, many working for less than half of the award rate. Under the Regulations attached to the *Aborigines Act* they had no industrial protection (Regulation 68). Not only could the Director decide how much an employer should pay his worker, he could also order that a proportion of it be paid to the District

Officer, to be spent on the Aborigine and his family as the officer 'deemed fit' (Regulation 67). There was also a provision for a man to be declared a 'slow worker' (Regulation 69), which meant that he could be paid at an even lesser rate. In spite of my efforts the unions showed no interest in changing this situation.

The conditions in the canteen where the Aborigines were forced to drink were hardly conducive to civilised drinking. It was housed in a beachfront building with little paint left on its walls, many broken windows, and large holes in the walls through which the wind screamed in. Rows of bent and buckled steel chairs, welded together, were the only seating. Drinkers had to collect their ration of four cans all at once; but even this was an improvement on the time, not so long before, when the cans had had to be opened at the counter. The toilets below the building had been condemned, and the nearest alternatives, across a football field, had no lights. It was little wonder, then, that the blacks complained bitterly about not having the same access to alcohol as the whites, or the right to take it home.

As regards hygiene, too, the State's laws were ignored as far as blacks were concerned. On seeing one day that their groceries — soap, bread, fruit, and anything else — were all thrown together in a bag, I decided to take a stand. Taking a loaf from Tommy, a customer I knew who was waiting to be served, I went to the checkout and insisted that it be wrapped, telling the manager that it was a contravention of the State's laws for him to let it go out of the shop unwrapped. He thought I was an inspector and soon complied. For a few days the blacks had their bread wrapped too. The hygiene, however, was not the only concern — more serious was the shortage of supplies. There was never enough to go round. And fruit, milk — everything — came over from the mainland only twice a week, on Tuesdays and Thursdays. How could anyone expect the children to be healthy?

The liquor rules and the hopelessness of the people led to many problems. Much of the little money they had went on black-market booze. Wine, which was smuggled onto the island in the most ingenious ways, sold for fifty dollars a bottle; for rum, whisky and other spirits, the seller could name his price, and get it. Many, though, drank methylated spirits; it sold for twenty-five dollars a bottle. These conditions led to abuse: fights broke out between men and men, between men and women, and between women and women. In many cases the problem was made worse because of the composition of the population.

On and off, about seven tribes lived — were forced to live — on Palm Island. These were made up of the tribes which were transferred to the island from other reserves. These differing tribes had different cultures and, to a lesser degree, different customs. The males and females of these different tribes communicated all right and the males took exception to this and quite often (nearly always, in fact) resentment would turn into violence to both parties. Call it 'revenge', 'resentment', 'jealousy' or simply tribal tradition. When taking this type of 'pay-back', knives were commonly used and murder was no stranger to Palm Island! Then, of course, there were the descendants of the original Palm Island inhabitants themselves. They were the core and they resented the intrusion of 'foreigners' most of all. But under the Act, they just had to live with it, like all the rest of the residents.

As on all Aboriginal reserves, the Government could order black men and women to give up their children. When one woman's children were taken ('for their own good') and placed in the island's dormitory, she fought in every way she knew to have them returned, but when all her efforts ended in failure she covered herself with kerosene and set herself alight. She died in agony. Iris Clay told me some years later that five women had died this way on the island, one the wife of Bill Congoo, with whom I had been quite friendly during my stay. What a terrible memory to be left with!

The attitudes of police (both black and white) also led to many injustices. One man was dragged from his bed one night and left handcuffed all night. A screaming black girl was taken from her home and tossed into gaol, where she was raped by four police officers. Some men on the island later took this as a licence to treat her the same way. When another girl — only fourteen years old and pregnant — was unable to give them information they were after, police took her and the coming baby's clothes; when she broke into the police station to get them back, she was arrested for breaking and entering. The list goes on.

Since there was no chance of getting mainland newspapers to publicise the people's plight, I suggested to Fred that we publish a newsletter of our own. We called it *Smoke Signal*. It gave us a forum, but also helped Fred let the island's people know what he was trying to achieve. We produced it regularly each week for about six months, charging ten cents a copy.

In the nine months that I was on the island, I talked to people about their lives, and wrote it all down. From them I got a picture of what they and their families had had to put up with, both growing up in various parts of Queensland, and on the island. I also started a branch of the Labor Party, and had a minor part in getting some oyster beds going.

During this time I got to know many of the children on the island, and found them outgoing, full of fun and friendly. I also got to know Fred and his family better. Their eldest son, Ricky, wasn't on the island at the time; he was in the United States, learning about the American Indians. But the other boys, Henry, Assam and Alfie were there, and so were their three daughters, Elizabeth, Nora and Bethel.

Not long before I was ready to leave the island, some of Fred's opponents got up a petition and had him dismissed from the council. Fred had never been popular with the authorities: he often bucked the system, and was reprimanded for it, but having such a large following and much support on the island, he had got away with a lot of it. Even the Aboriginal Council itself had no real power: any decisions they made had to be approved by the authorities, but were often ignored.

When I left Palm Island I was still unaware of the great changes the visit was to bring in my life. On the personal side, the effects were to some extent indirect. After I returned to Brisbane, Lillian and I gradually developed different interests: I was concerned with Aboriginal interests, and with my new career, while Lillian was more interested in women's rights. We each 'did our own thing': soon we drifted apart and eventually split up. I had another shot at marriage — with Sandra, an Aboriginal girl I had met on Palm Island — but this lasted only a very short time, and once again I was alone.

On the working front, though, I have never looked back. I wrote of my experiences of Palm Island, and my book, *This is Palm Island*, was published by the then Australian Institute of Aboriginal Studies in Canberra in 1978. The Institute later commissioned me to interview and record the experiences of Aborigines in far-west Queensland which resulted in *Dreamtime Nightmares* (1985); my third book, *Up Rode the Troopers*, was published by University of Queensland Press in 1990.

My research for *Dreamtime Nightmares* enabled me to renew my friendship with Fred and Iris Clay. After they were forced from the island around 1979, when authorities ordered their son Rick to leave, they lived for a while in Redcliffe, near Brisbane, but Fred was now a field officer at Mt Isa for the Commonwealth Department of Aboriginal Affairs, and Iris was living in Charters Towers. I talked to them separately of their lives before and on Palm Island (see *Dreamtime Nightmares*), but became very concerned about the state of Iris's health. She died in the early 1980s, and Fred died shortly afterwards.

Years slipped quickly and silently by. I continued to keep in contact with Palm Island until one day, during a phone call, Fred Clay's son Rick, who was now the Chairman of the Palm Island Aboriginal

Chapter Four

Council, requested me to pay the island another visit. It seemed that the old faction fighting had erupted again. I assured him I'd be up as soon as possible, and several days later found myself walking once more on the soft, white sands of Palm Island. Once again the cold, blue water was washing over my feet as the waves broke just a few metres off shore. Behind me were the screeches and happy squeals of young black children as they played among the rocks just off the beach. As I looked around I could see the familiar sights of several semi-clad men sleeping on the warm sand, each with an empty wine flagon beside him. Above me I could see the aircraft that had brought me across from Townsville about an hour earlier, its propeller flogging the wind as it made its slow progress back to the mainland.

Chapter 5

I wondered idly what I would find on the island this time: would the racism of the past still be evident? Would there still be the wild, drunken brawls of the 1970s? Would the noses of the kids still flow with that yellow, streaky mucous which seemed to afflict all the kids here? Would methylated spirits still cost twenty-five dollars a bottle on the black market?

I rolled my trouser legs back down and, gripping my suitcase, headed towards the shop. I saw the people sitting on the retaining wall alongside the Administration Building, just as they had always sat. Nobody ever talked much: they just sat and watched the passing parade of people doing their shopping, and the kids playing on the roadway; or nodded off under the warm sun; or waited for the pub to open. Occasionally a fight would break out, preceded by, 'Give me that fuckin' grog, ya bastard! Get ya own fuckin' grog.'

The old, familiar hall, its walls literally covered with the names of people and Cupid's hearts with arrows and initials in them, had been burnt down. Nobody knew ' 'ow it 'appened', but the kids had got the blame. The old tower clock still stood in the park, showing the same time as it had that day in 1974 when I first arrived on Palm Island. This was the clock which, I was told then, ' 'asn't gone since Christ was a boy'. It was to have been repaired but I was told that the repairer, the local blacksmith, had died.

I was glad to be back; it would be good to see all my old friends again. But somehow the atmosphere didn't seem to be the same. The men appeared to be quieter: they just moped around. The women, too, were different. They no longer flashed their brilliant smiles as they walked along, greeting their friends. Something seemed terribly wrong on Palm Island. Certainly, a new building program had been taking place since the abolition, in 1984, of the Queensland *Aborigines Act*, but still the people appeared mindless. I asked a few of the residents the reason for this.

'Too much fuckin' grog.'

This was the response of every person I asked. Since I had last been there, a new canteen (really a pub) had been built and, with the Act rescinded, limitless alcohol in all its forms was readily available. I have always campaigned for equal drinking rights for Aborigines but, after witnessing its results, I'm not so sure I was on the right track.

My first call was to the Aboriginal Council office. Rick Clay and I shook hands firmly. He had been only a lad when I last saw him; now he was Chairman of the Council, a strapping young man and as strong as a bull. He stood about 178 centimetres tall and his shoulders were square and firm. Although his face was cleanshaven, his lips were outlined with a circular moustache and a beard. After a while I asked him why he had wanted me to come up to give him support.

'I need the newsletter (*Smoke Signal*) to help create unity on Palm Island,' he told me. 'There are some people here who want to cause trouble. I'm sick and tired of all this faction fighting.'

'Why would they want to cause trouble?' I asked him.

He explained that some of these people wanted to lease a part of the island known as Wallaby Point and set up a tourist resort. 'But we'll talk about that later,' he said.

'Where am I going to stay?' I asked him. 'Any ideas?' He rolled his tongue around in his cheeks before answering.

'Well,' he said at last, 'I'm stuck for room right now. I've got some visitors that arrived without notice.' He scratched his chin for a moment in thought. 'I reckon young Assam would have stacks of room,' he continued. Assam was his younger brother and lived in an area of the island known as 'the farm'. The last time I had seen Assam was at the hostel in Redcliffe where his parents were caretakers. He was only about knee-high then, but when I met him a little later in the day I found that he, too, had grown into a barrel-chested young man. I told him what his brother Rick had said about putting me up.

'No worries,' he smiled. 'There's plenty of room here.' He ushered me into a room in which stood a soft, vacant bed. I placed my suitcase on the floor and walked back out into the kitchen where the inevitable pot of tea was standing. I felt I had known Assam for long enough so I put my smokes down on the table and took the liberty of pouring myself a mug of tea. As I stood beside the kitchen table, a slim young man with a weedy moustache walked in.

'Don't ya' know me, Bill?' he said familiarly. I looked at him carefully. His face was vaguely familiar but I had no idea who he was. His face widened into a smile.

'I'm Henry,' he informed me. I looked at him more intently now. Henry Clay, as I remembered him, was a skinny-legged kid who was always sniffing.

'Jesus Christ! So you are.' I found it difficult to believe that such a skinny kid could have grown up into such a fine, well-proportioned young man.

We spent the next hour or so reliving the past, and they brought me up to date with the recent happenings on Palm Island. Time was getting on a bit so I decided to go for a walk down to the village, hoping, perhaps, to bump into a few old friends. I picked my packet of smokes up from the table; they had copped a bashing during the past hour or so. I told the Clays where I was going and walked out of the room and down the flight of steps.

As I neared the village I saw my old friend Billy Congoo. How thin he had become. I walked over to where he was standing under a scraggy old tree. He recognised me immediately.

'You old bastard!' he greeted me, holding out his bony hand. 'What the fuck are you doin' back 'ere?'

'Good-day, Bill,' I said. 'You look a bit crook. What's the matter?' He screwed up his face in disgust.

'Ah,' he replied, nodding towards the hotel, 'too much fuckin' grog. Christ, I don't know where I am half the time.' He gave the kind of chuckle that only Billy Congoo could give. Unkempt and slightly dirty, old Billy was a nice bloke, even though he was a pisspot.

'Ah, Bill,' I said, looking him over. 'You'll have to give the grog and those smokes away. You'll end up — '

'Hey, look out!' he laughed. 'You'd do better talkin' to that fuckin' tree there.'

We sat down together on a piece of coconut palm trunk that had been cut into lengths. We yarned on for a while, but every few minutes he would look across to where the pub stood with its doors tantalisingly closed. I knew that the instant those doors opened our conversation would come to an abrupt end. He licked his lips repeatedly.

'What do you think of the place now, Bill?' I asked him. 'I notice a lot of new buildings here now.'

He rolled his head to one side as he thought out his answer.

'Well, Bill,' he replied, 'the trouble is, the place is moving too fast. Too fast for the people, you know?'

'But, bloody hell,' I replied. 'We moaned and complained until we got these things — like the rights to take grog home, to have access to grog in the same manner as the white man and to be able to come and go from the island without a permit. You should be happier now.'

Bill remained silent. He stared at the ground as he reflected on my words. He was about to speak when the sound of a bolt being pulled back stopped him. The bar door was being opened and, as I had suspected, our conversation was at an end. Bill rose, brushed some imaginary dirt from his trousers, and headed for the bar.

'Well, see ya later,' he tossed back over his shoulder.

'Yeah, Bill,' I replied, 'see you later.' I don't condemn Bill; he had a lot of problems. Undoubtedly he was still thinking about the suicide of his wife when her kids were taken from her. Bill had a lot of mates waiting for the pub to open. They weren't all men, either.

After a little while I strolled over to the pub and went in. It was certainly a modern, well-planned hotel. In one corner stood a pool table and in another a huge television set; its signal (from Sky Channel) was collected by two large satellite dishes on the roof of the building. It appeared to me that Palm Island was going ahead in leaps and bounds, so much so that I began to wonder why Ricky Clay was worried. I decided to go back to the office and have a talk to him.

Almost immediately, he returned to the subject of the tourist resort. 'It has already been signed up,' he told me. 'All that is needed is just one more signature.'

'What can you do about it?' I asked him. 'If that's what the people want then surely that's it.'

'That's one of the reasons I need *Smoke Signal*,' he replied.

'Why don't you call a community meeting? That's the way to go,' I advised him. 'That's how your father, Fred, would have handled it. Any time there was unrest in the camp, he would call a meeting to put any ugly rumours to rest.'

Rick placed a forefinger to the tip of his nose, obviously thinking deeply about what I had just said. 'I'll call a meeting,' he said, as he suddenly swung himself up out of his chair. 'I've wanted to do this, but I had no support. I feel better now that you're here.'

I must admit that I was at a loss to know what difference I would make. I had had no real contact with the island for years and, although I was well known there, I certainly had no clout in the politics of the place.

Something was wrong somewhere. I had no idea what was afoot, but something sure was. I decided to tread carefully and watch my back. I made arrangements to call at Rick's house that evening to talk over the strategy we should follow in producing the new series of *Smoke Signal*. I busied myself for the remainder of the day by collecting statements and typing up a possible format for the newsletter.

Chapter 6

That night, after having dinner with Assam, which consisted of a delicious turtle steak, I strolled across to Rick's house, as arranged. Rick invited me inside, but then his behaviour and his attitude absolutely astounded me.

'You know, Bill,' he started out, 'I don't think you're the same person Dad knew. I don't think you're genuine.' I looked at him in disbelief. '*What?*' was all I could manage to say.

'You're only here to get material for a book. You're not interested in the people.' He pointed to my wristwatch. 'You've got a fancy watch, a tape-recorder. You only want to write a book about this place.'

Well, my 'fancy watch' cost $32 and the tape-recorder was the property of the then Australian Institute of Aboriginal Studies in Canberra. Actually, I hadn't been in the slightest bit interested in writing a book but, by Christ, I was now! I couldn't believe what I was hearing. Could this really be the son of Fred Clay? The only way I could defend myself was to offer to show him what I had already written for the newsletter. He allowed his wife, who is a gem of a woman, to accompany me to Assam's house to collect the material which was to prove my 'sincerity'. After reading the material, which portrayed Rick as above reproach, he agreed that I was vindicated.

'I had to find out,' he said, as he put his hand on my shoulder. He turned to his wife and said to her, 'Well, I think he's passed the acid test.' He looked at me again. 'It hurt me as much as it hurt you,' he said.

Bullshit! I wasn't hurt; I felt a great feeling of repugnance. I'm afraid my belief in the credibility of Ricky Clay fell sharply that night. Be that as it may, he was a man who oozed sincerity and warmth and I got the feeling that his dedication was beyond question.

But why had he pulled such a childish stunt?

I rose early next morning and walked the short distance into the village. As I neared the hotel I noticed a man and a woman sitting on a seat outside. I crossed over to them. I didn't recognise the woman for a while, but suddenly the memory came flooding back. 'You're the girl who came to my caravan one night, years ago, complaining of a sore stomach,' I said to her.

It had been fourteen years ago. She looked closely at me, not daring to speak to an apparent stranger. Then her face lit up with recognition. 'Hey! You — you Bill Rosser, eh?'

I smiled at her excitement. She stood up shakily and gave me a light hug, then she laughed out loud. 'Hey, you know what? That night when I come to you, you take me to the hospital, you remember?'

'Yes, I remember,' I replied. 'You were in a mess that night.'

'You know what happen?' she asked me as she sat down again beside the man whom I now recognised as her father.

I shook my head. 'No, but you were pretty crook, I know that. They kept you in hospital, didn't they? I remember your father waiting outside for you.'

'I had a miscarriage,' she said, quietly and confidentially. 'I nearly die.' She stood up again and put her arms around me. 'You know what? I think I would have died if you hadn't taken me to the hospital in your car.' I looked down at her father, who was trying to speak. His voice was slurred and his left arm hung down uselessly. He wasn't drunk but looked as if he might have suffered a stroke at some time. He made no attempt to get up.

'Hey,' the girl said, 'you want a drink?' I shook my head.

'Aw, no thanks,' I declined her hospitality. 'See, I'm on these tablets and I'm not allowed to drink.' It was a harmless lie that had got me out of similar situations several times in the past.

'Where you stay?' she asked me. I told her where I was camped and that I was quite happy there.

'If you don't like that place you can come to our house,' she offered. She lifted her arm and pointed to a brown-roofed house a little way up the road.

'Plenty of room there,' she explained. ' Only my father and me live there.'

'What's it like living here now? Is it any better?'

'What you mean, "better"?'

'Well, now that the Act has gone, you seem to have reasonable drinking rights,' I said to her. 'The houses are well-built. You must be better off.'

She cupped her chin in her hands for a while, then turned to her father. 'What you reckon?' she asked him. 'Is it better now?'

He mumbled something unintelligible. 'Ah, you wouldn't know,' she told him, unkindly. 'I don't know, either. Too much grog though,' she added.

She noticed the camera hanging off my wrist. There seems to be nothing Aborigines, particularly the kids, like more than to have their photos taken.

'You take my phota?' she asked. Without any further prompting, I took a picture of her and her poor, wretched father sitting on the seat outside that pub. She attempted a smile which, without doubt, had been a very pretty smile years before, but there was no way the camera was going to lie about her missing teeth. But she was happy.

As the morning wore on I met many of my friends of old. They had one thing in common; before they said hello they bit me for a smoke. Invariably each had 'given mine away to a mate' who, in turn, had given his away to another mate. But somehow everybody got a smoke.

Later I met Bill Congoo again. Maybe he'd fallen asleep the previous night with a cigarette in his hand because his shirt now contained cigarette holes that hadn't been there when I last saw him.

'Jesus! Got a smoke, Bill?' were his first words to me, even before he had crossed the road.

'Aw, Bill,' I teased him, 'you know bloody well I don't smoke.' His face screwed up as I spoke the words, but seconds later his tobacco-stained teeth appeared in a smile as I pulled out my packet of cigarettes.

'You bastard, you!' he said, good-naturedly. 'You'd tell me shit was honey, wouldn't you?'

I had made arrangements the previous night to meet Rick in his office that morning but it was still pretty early, so I wandered back to Assam's place for some more smokes. I was certain to need them. When I arrived, he and several of his friends were trying to piece together a new child's swing Assam's wife, Delphine, had bought in Townsville. It was an automatic contraption which, when wound up with a cranking handle, caused the swing to go to and fro for a considerable length of time. After a lot of assembling and disassembling and several unaccounted-for nuts and bolts, they got the thing to work. Assam placed the youngster in the seat and wound it up. I really don't know who got the most entertainment from it, the baby or the spectators, me included. But it was a gem of an idea. Still, Delphine wasn't at all happy when she returned from a friend's place and saw it.

'You silly buggers,' she reproved, 'you've got it back-to-front. The brand name should be facing the front. You're a hopeless lot of fellas!' Even though we all explained to her that it didn't matter which side the 'bloody brand' was on, when the others went away and left Delphine to her own devices, she reassembled it 'the *right* bloody way'. I really don't think it worked quite as well though. Soon Assam returned with the boot of his old car packed with dry wood. As they had an electric stove, I enquired about the need for the wood.

'Old Assam is having a birthday today,' he explained. 'We're going to put on a barbecue for him.'

Old Assam, or 'Sugar' as he was affectionately called, was no relation to Assam Clay, and was getting on in years. I don't know what his exact age was, but he would have been well over eighty. He was sitting under the house, trying to put on a T-shirt he had received as a birthday present. As he wasn't familiar with this type of attire, he had put it on back-to-front and inside out. A couple of kids came up and, after laughing at the old man's dilemma, helped him to put the shirt on correctly. This in itself was an hilarious spectacle. He smiled sheepishly as he stood up to display the garment. We all clapped at his successful donning of the shirt.

Old he might have been, but his fragility didn't stop him from putting a much younger man in his place at the pub one day. This man said something to which the old man took exception and, without further ado, old Assam proceeded to thump the objectionable one. Down he went! Old Assam had to be held in check by his son Moa. He cooled down and eventually shook the offender, who was spitting blood, by the hand.

But back to the barbecue. To cut a long story short, it rained heavily that day and persisted throughout the next several days. Needless to say, Assam is still waiting for his birthday barbecue. Well, maybe next year.

As we sat under the house out of the rain, I spoke to another acquaintance from my visit to the island in 1974. I only ever knew him as 'Cotter'. A serious man who was dedicated to the advancement of Palm Island, he echoed the words of most of the other Palm Islanders I spoke to.

'We're moving too fast, Bill,' he said, earnestly. 'It's going to take these people a long time to get over the conditions that were enforced on them by the Act. They just can't get up and change their lifestyle overnight ... it'll take time.' Like many other older Palm Islanders, Cotter grasped the situation well. Many Palm Island blacks claimed it could take three or even four generations for them to overcome the trauma of the intense racism that existed under the Act. But Cotter held out some hope for the future.

'When the Act was repealed,' he said, 'they [the Department of Aboriginal and Islander Affairs (DAIA)] came over and smashed all our oyster beds. They don't *want* blacks to be successful.'

When I lived on the island before, there had been a thriving oyster farm there. I had assisted, in a small way, in setting it up. A specialist had come over from Magnetic Island to advise and supervise the project. Now it was all gone, smashed! Who was responsible for ruining the oyster beds, I do not know. I *do* know that the blacks had put in a hell of a lot of work on the enterprise. I found it difficult to believe that the DAIA had anything to do with its destruction but the blacks are adamant.

Cotter lit a smoke and blew a blue cloud into the air.

'You know,' he remarked, 'I'd like to see a whole lot more employment here. The people have nothing to do.'

'But, Cotter,' I asked, quietly, 'if employment was available here, would the blokes do the work? Or would they idle their time away in the pub?'

He thought for a while, dragging heavily on his cigarette. He was clearly offended by my question.

'Well,' he said, pulling a face, 'there would be some people who wouldn't work. You get that anywhere.'

He was quite correct, of course. I know some white people — strong young bucks — who would not work in an iron lung! And they will tell you so.

Our conversation was interrupted by the skinniest cat I have ever seen. It came in from the road and walked languidly to the area under the house where we were sitting. I really am not exaggerating when I tell you that it was no more than one inch across its back. It stopped in front of Cotter and simply collapsed in a heap. We looked at each other in amazement. How could a cat so thin still be alive? We were unsure whether to go and get it something to eat or to carry it back across the road. We ended up doing neither. As we laughed at the impossible sight, the cat stirred, rose up and wandered back whence it had come.

'The rain has eased a bit,' Cotter observed. 'I think I'll go and see what's happening downtown.' He rose from his seat and headed down towards the township.

Moments later, I decided to follow. As I was passing the pub, one of the women I'd been talking to earlier called me over. As I approached she held out a stubbie of beer.

'Here,' she invited, 'have a sip. You look hot.' Actually, I *was* feeling a bit hot, regardless of the break in the weather.

'Bloody oath,' I took the bottle from her. 'I wouldn't mind a mouthful.' I lifted the bottle to my lips and took a decent swig. But something wasn't right: this wasn't the way Fourex used to taste. At first I thought it might be because the beer was hot. I smacked my lips, and then it dawned on me: the beer was heavily laced with methylated spirits! This surprised me because now that the Act was a thing of the past, I hadn't thought there'd be any need to drink metho. There were plenty of spirits readily available at the pub. I spat it out hurriedly.

'Ahhh, fuck!' I expostulated, gasping for breath. 'What's this shit?' She threw an embarrassed look over to the pub.

'Shhh,' she whispered. 'Don't tell the fuckin' world!'

I grimaced but said nothing further. I didn't want to embarrass her in front of the group of men standing in front of the pub. I handed the bottle back to her and she took a swig.

'Thanks,' I said, quietly. My thanks, however, were most insincere.

I stayed talking to her for a while, then wandered off towards the shopping centre. It crossed my mind that I mustn't stand too close to anybody I was speaking to or I would be sure to get a reputation as a metho drinker. My breath reeked of the stuff and every time I breathed in I almost suffocated. What ghastly stuff!

When I entered the shop, it occurred to me that the supply boat mustn't be in yet. All that was in the fruit section were a few spotted tomatoes and a discoloured cabbage. Other than that, the shop was well-stocked with groceries, clothing and kitchenware.

As I gazed idly at the rows of tins on the shelves, an elderly man touched me on the elbow.

'Good-day,' he greeted me. 'Jeez, I never thought I'd see you over this way again.' He held out a gnarled old hand which I took and held firmly. I have vivid memories of this man: it was he who, on my last visit, had given me the loaf of bread in the shop when I told him the bread should be wrapped. He remembered the episode too, and laughed as he mentioned it to me.

'You didn't laugh the day you gave me the bread,' I chided. 'You were shit scared, eh?' He subdued his laughter and lowered his eyes.

'Aw, no, Bill,' he admitted, sheepishly. 'I thought we'd get our arses kicked off the island that day.' We both burst out laughing again. He threw several glances towards the pub and I gathered he wanted to make a polite departure.

Chapter Six 45

'Listen, I've got to do some shopping,' I lied.

That was all the excuse he needed. 'Aw, right-oh, Bill,' he threw over his shoulder as he took off. 'I'd better not keep you.' I smiled inwardly at his artlessness, but before I could reply, he was striding energetically down the road in the direction of the pub.

It was time now for me to go across to the Aboriginal Council rooms and have a yarn to Chairman Rick Clay. Through the huge glass window of his office, Rick had seen me coming and as I entered he nodded me to a chair on the opposite side of his desk.

'I'm glad about this meeting I've set up,' he informed me. 'I've wanted to call a community meeting but I felt that I was on my own — you know.' I looked at him but didn't return his smile. He appeared to be experiencing some mental conflict as he nervously toyed with a pencil.

'What do you mean, "on your own"?' I enquired.

'Well,' he replied, rubbing the flat of his hand on the top of his desk, 'I need some sort of support. Now that you're here I feel much better. I know that you will give me the support I need. That's why I need a newsletter.'

He seemed to relax somewhat as I smiled briefly. I was at a loss to understand why he placed so much dependence on me when I hadn't visited the island for fourteen years, and I told him so.

'But you worked with Dad,' he said. 'He trusted you all the way. That's how I know I can trust you.'

'But for Christ sake, trust me for *what*?' I replied. 'The people here elected *you*. Surely you can trust them now!' He shook his head in seeming despair.

'Bill,' he explained, 'nothing is confidential at our meetings. Do you know that within an hour of when we finish our meetings the other faction knows exactly what was discussed and everything that went on?' He threw his hands in the air. 'They know everything that is said.'

When I asked him how this could be, he told me that one of the councillors was friendly with the opposition.

'He's a mole,' Rick said.

'Well,' I asked him, 'can't the loyal councillors vote him out?'

'No,' he replied.

'Why not?'

'Because the people voted him in. You know, if Palm Island had solidarity and unity, it could become the convention centre of the world.' His confidence was returning. His eyes gleamed with the fire I had often seen in his father's eyes. I waited for him to continue.

'If only we could get the people here to unite,' he said. 'If only we could live in harmony, we'd be on top of the world.' I thought about his words for a while.

'Rick,' I advised him, 'the only way you're going to get the confidence, the respect and the understanding of the people is to hold public meetings. You must let the people have their say. You must listen to the people. That is our way. It has always been our way.'

He thought deeply for a while.

'Yes,' he replied, 'I realise that. I know you've got to motivate the people, I know that.' He looked me firmly in the eye. 'But who's going to motivate the motivator?' The question was a good one, but I had to admit I had no answer. He smiled at winning his point.

'Do you think this newsletter will unite the people?'

'Oh yes,' he replied, but with an anxious look. 'That's the whole idea. And you are the one who can do it. You did it for Dad.'

His utterance sobered me. I felt I wasn't worthy of such acclaim. Fred and I had worked together. It was certainly a challenge but we had enjoyed every minute of it.

'Rick, there is one thing we must be careful of,' I warned him, 'we must ensure that our newsletter doesn't just become a vehicle for demagoguery. It's essential to let the people have their say.'

'What do you mean?'

'Well, we must encourage public input,' I explained. 'I think the best way to do that would be through a Letters to the Editor column.'

Rick agreed that this would indeed be a good way of finding out the complaints and concerns of the Palm Island people. 'That's just what I want to do,' he said. 'I want to find out their problems.'

'Can't you find out at public meetings?'

'Not really,' he replied, 'because a lot of the people will not voice their problems, or disapproval, publicly because they are afraid of being jeered at or ostracised.' I could understand that: it's not all that easy living on a small island with people of differing tribal customs and cultures.

'Tell me, Rick,' I changed the subject, 'what became of all those oyster beds that were here when I left? They should be thriving by now. Was it the DAIA?'

'No,' Rick replied. 'That was the Department of Community Services, or the Department of Ethnic Affairs, I believe. They change their names that many fucking times!' He laughed mirthlessly as he answered my question. 'They're the ones responsible for it.'

Chapter Six   47

Rick and I talked for some considerable time until eventually the subject got back to the newsletter, which was becoming a touchy subject with me.

As it happened, I had come to the island at the time the Palm Island footballers were to receive their credits and trophies, and was looking forward to attending the function that night and perhaps to capture some of the presentations with my video camera. I had taken it over with me with the idea of taking some footage to show later for friends in the city. However, like many of my plans, these, too, went awry. At about 3 o'clock in the afternoon the rain began to pelt down again. Rain? Strike a light, you've never seen rain like it! I was standing on Assam's verandah and it was impossible to see the roadway. Papers and people's belongings were blowing all around the area. Dogs, which had been languidly stretched out in the various yards, took off for cover. Coconut palms bent almost double before the force of the wind. Well, there was no way in the world I was going to walk the two miles or so down to the township in this weather. Bugger the football presentation.

I later learned that, because of the rain, the presentation wasn't very well attended, which was a pity because the organisers had gone to great lengths to make the night a success. They had prepared stacks of food which, according to one of the young men I spoke to the following day, consisted of turtle, pork, chicken, goat and heaps of vegetables.

'I needed that turtle, too,' the young man joked.

'Why? Were you that hungry?' I asked.

'Aw, no,' he replied, 'but I haven't shit for a few days now. That turtle meat makes you go pretty quick.' He grinned as he looked for corroboration from several other young men who were present. They smiled and nodded in agreement.

'Aw, too right,' one of them remarked. 'That's one of the side effects of turtle; you can eat too much of it.'

One of the men present was Moa, old Assam's son. I had difficulty remembering his correct name for a while, and continually called him 'Noah'.

'Not fucking Noah,' he chided me. 'It's fucking M-O-A!' We all broke into loud laughter at his frustration. He got his point across, though: I called him by his correct name from then on.

Moa was, to my mind, the most likeable young fellow on Palm Island: his ready laugh, keen sense of humour and good nature left little to be desired in a companion. He was tall and well built, and was certainly a powerful man. He had the rare capacity to be a serious conversationalist when he needed to be and was also endowed with a tremendous sense of humour: his ready wit was a joy to listen to. His full name was Moa Sam. We became quite good friends during my short stay on the island. He had his own ideas about the running of the island, but I think, in the long run, his plans for the future of the community were much the same as Rick Clay's. The only difference was that he had a different and quieter way of attaining those goals.

'Things move too fast for these fellows,' he said to me. 'Sure, they want self-determination and security, but at their own pace.'

'How do you mean "their own pace", Moa?'

'Well,' he replied with hesitation, 'you see all the new buildings, the new houses, the hotel, Sky Channel? It's too much at once. See, although the standards on Palm Island have changed, the attitudes of the people aren't changing with them. They need more time — their own time.' I pondered his words for a few moments.

'Yes, but hang on, Moa,' I argued. 'You jokers wanted to get rid of the Act. You wanted improved living conditions. So now, you've got them and you're still not happy!' Moa seemed a bit frustrated, not at my remarks but at my seeming inability to comprehend the slowness of the Palm Island people in changing from a life of terrible oppression to one of modern living and comparative luxury. We both looked at the ground, each waiting for the other to speak. After several minutes of silence, Moa could stand it no longer.

'Ah, fuck it!' he burst out. 'We won't solve anything here.' I smiled at the ease with which he changed the subject. Brutal, but effective.

Now our attention was drawn to a large car, towing an equally large boat.

'There he goes,' Moa remarked, with artificial disgust, 'the smallest man with the biggest boat.' He drew out the 'biggest' to add emphasis to his words.

The owner of the car and boat was Alfie, another member of the numerous Clay family. The youngest, I think. A small man, his pleasantness, his geniality and his sincerity far outweighed his size. He was also a gentle man. His hobby was fishing and when he took his huge boat out to sea, as he often did, you could never be quite sure what Alfie would come home with. It could be a turtle, a dugong or one of the largest fish in the ocean. Only the previous day he had returned with an enormous coral trout. His brother, Henry, had cooked the fish, then nonchalantly tossed it onto the kitchen table — a gesture he had perfected. Moa, who, of course, was a very good friend of Alfie's, often went out with him in the boat and on one occasion had returned with a large dugong. This catch was so popular that I didn't even get a smell of it! I was certainly caught napping that day.

Chapter 7

I awoke the following day to a morning that only Palm Island can produce. The weather had cleared and the sun was shining softly on the tips of the palms, creating millions of shimmering silver sequins as the breeze caught their pale-green leaves. The coconut trees took on a new appearance as the breeze rustled through their fronds. I rose and put the kettle on. I had some difficulty lighting the gas stove, and recalled Moa's words about 'modern' equipment. It struck me as strange (though not unacceptable) that a race of people who, not so very long ago, had cooked their food over an open wood fire should now be preparing their *haute cuisine* on a modern stove fuelled by gas.

After several cups of tea, I picked up my video camera and panned around the landscape as seen from Assam's front verandah. When I viewed the instant playback in the camera it occurred to me that it was fortunate I hadn't been filming a football match: I had taken some absolutely stunning footage of treetops, roofs and out-of-focus pedestrians. After some practice and reading the instruction manual (for the first time), I gradually got the hang of it. The experience gave me enough confidence to agree to video a dancing show that was to be performed later in the day for the benefit of expected tourists. I subsequently took the video pictures all right and, as it happened, they turned out really well. I must admit, though, that the 'corroborees' performed for the tourists would probably not have had a place of distinction in a tribal situation. Nevertheless the tourists clapped and the performers sniggered — another day, another dollar.

When I returned to Assam's house that afternoon, Assam was in a very agitated state.

'What's the matter?' I ventured to ask. 'You look upset.'

Assam fixed me with eyes that were watery with rage. I then realised that I had blundered upon some touchy subject. I followed his gaze as he looked towards his car, and the reason for his anger became obvious: the windscreen of his car had been shattered. I said something like 'Bloody hell!' or 'Shit!' Assam made up for my lack of words.

'Some dirty, rotten bastard put three rocks through my windscreen,' Assam screamed. 'By Christ! If I find the bastard that did it, I'll kill him. Look at it! Fucking glass everywhere. Where am I going to get another one?' Assam continued with his tirade for quite some time. His voice was loud enough to bring the neighbours out onto their front steps to listen to this lesson in profanity. As for me, I had to clamp my teeth together hard to avoid laughing out loud. Not at the fact that the windscreen was broken but at Assam's impassioned vituperation.

'Poor bastard,' I thought. I know from experience the emotional distress you can suffer at the sight of a broken windscreen and the anguish of seeing the culprit vehicle wag its arse at you as it disappears in a cloud of dust.

'Rotten bastard!' Assam was off again.

'Do you reckon you could get another one?' I asked weakly.

'Aw, Christ!' he exploded. 'Where the fuck am I going to get one in this arsehole of a place?' His face reddened again. Delphine was a wise wife: she remained indoors and said nothing.

Someone came to Assam's rescue later in the afternoon. As the car was a Holden, it wasn't difficult to take a windscreen out of one of the many wrecks on the island. Assam had just been too overcome at the sight of the busted-up windscreen to think straight. When they polished the glass, its brightness was eclipsed only by Assam's smile.

'Hey,' he called upstairs, 'you help me put it in, Henry?'

A groan issued from the sitting room and Henry stood up and peered over the verandah rail. Luckily, Moa was just coming in the gate, and the three of them soon fitted the newly acquired replacement. The smile returned to Assam's face once more.

As all the excitement was over and the comical howls of anguish had now ceased, I decided on a walk up to the township, hoping to take a few photographs. As I was passing an outcrop of rock on the beach I heard children laughing. I approached it, and peered over: about ten kids were jumping and splashing in the shallow water. They were having a great time, the sun glistening on their black, wet little bodies. It took a while to negotiate the rocks and uneven ground, and when I finally reached the playing children, they had already seen me; so my idea of taking a few candid photographs went begging.

'Hey,' one of the bolder kids yelled to me, 'you take my phota? I'll smile.' The offer of a smile made it evident that they were well-versed in the ways of tourists. I removed my camera from its bag and proceeded to take some delightful photographs of these lovely, happy children. Like all the younger kids on Palm Island, they were very friendly and anxious to speak to anyone who approached them in a friendly manner. They were a bit shy at first, but as I got talking to them, their reserve left them and a more enchanting group of kids you could never find. They were all skinny and several of them had sores on their legs, but it didn't seem to bother them.

'You come over on a boat?' one boy asked.

'Nah,' I replied, mock disgust, 'I live here.'

'Where you bin live, eh?' he quizzed.

'Down at the farm,' I informed him. 'Down with Assam — Assam Clay.' They looked at each other silently, asking each other if they should know me.

'Hey,' the questioner smiled, 'I not seen you dere. You gammon.' I smiled at the typical sideways glance with which an Aborigine can imbue so many nuances.

'No, I not gammon,' I replied. 'I used to live here years ago. You weren't even a twinkle in your father's eye then.' They came and scrambled around me, sitting on the rocks in expectation of having a yarn with me. One lad happened to slip and landed heavily on his bum. He let slip a naughty word and the others lost no time in chastising him. The offender hung his head.

'Hey,' the others reproved, 'you a Christian. You don't say that word.' The boy remained silent and drew his knees up under his chin in embarrassment.

'Are you all Christians?' I asked.

'Yes,' they answered in unison, 'we all Christians people here. We good boys.'

'You mean none of you swear or tell fibs?' I challenged. They all shook their innocent little heads vigorously. I couldn't help smiling at their sincerity and innocence.

'To be a true Christian,' I explained to them, 'you must not swear, or tell lies, or cheat.'

'No, we don't,' they answered.

'You must be good to your mum and dad, too. And go to church.'

'Oh, yes, we do all that,' they assured me. The boy who had been admonished by his fellows looked up at me.

'Can you chuck rocks at cars?' he asked. I exploded into laughter, not at the question but at the seriousness with which it was asked.

'No, you're not allowed to do that,' I replied.

'Aw, shit!' was the disappointed response. The other kids chided him again but I don't think it had any effect. I felt sure they had a traitor within the group.

'There's a lot more to being a Christian than not telling lies and swearing,' I said to them. 'You've got to help your fellow man and share with him.'

'Eh? What do you mean?' the boy with the sore leg asked. I found it extremely difficult to conceal my amusement.

'Well, if you have an ice-cream, or twenty dollars, you've got to share it with your friends and neighbours. Otherwise you're just pretending to be Christians.'

Their expressions of superiority changed to ones of chagrin.

'Aw, fuck that,' one of them spat out, all Christian thoughts erased from his little mind. He looked back to another of the group and pointed at him. 'You wouldn't give me half of that mango yesterday, fuck ya.'

If these kids were going to have a brawl, I wasn't anxious to be around. I placed my camera back in its bag, and began to make off.

'You sure 'bout that?' another kid asked me, a puzzled frown covering his face.

'Yep,' I called back. 'No doubt about it.' I left the astonished young swimmers, and they watched me as I disappeared behind the outcrop of rock. I smiled and shook my head in amusement. I hoped I hadn't disillusioned them too much about the Christian faith.

When I arrived back at Assam's house I discovered what looked like a dead body on the settee. A tall, slim man in his early thirties was lying quite straight as if he had been carefully positioned. His arms, which were long and thin, were close to his sides, as were his legs, toes pointing directly upwards. His face wore a five o'clock shadow and his greyish-brown hair was a tousled mat. His face bore light, clean lines and his aquiline nose almost belied his Aboriginal extraction. He was quite pallid. As I watched him, wondering how he had died and who had placed him on the settee, two watery eyes half-opened and a foot moved slightly. Still convinced he was a cadaver, I jumped back quickly. There was, in fact, another reason for distancing myself from the form: his legs were quite close to a most sensitive part of my body. I spoke to the form but received no reply. I carefully bent over the unkempt head and sniffed gently. The mystery was fully explained.

The following morning the 'corpse' returned to the land of the living, so to speak. His name was Jamie. His line of work was bull-catching, he told me. He was a very likeable young fellow and very friendly, with a smile that started at the corner of his mouth and spread until a full set of even teeth were exposed.

'What do you mean "bull-catching"?' I asked him. Jamie shrugged his shoulders at my question. He gave the impression that it was quite simple and that everybody should know how to catch bulls.

'Ah, well,' he began to explain, 'I got a truck with big steel pipes on it.' He made the shape of the pipes with his hands. 'See, this pipe,' he continued, 'it's got a big hook on it. What I do is, I chase the bull until I've got 'im buggered — that is, I've got 'im knocked up — then I work the truck closer to him until the hook gets him around the arse, see.' He drew out a well-used plastic pouch which contained the last of his tobacco and proceeded to roll a smoke. I was hoping that my packet of cigarettes wasn't making a telltale bulge in my pocket.

'The trick,' he resumed, 'is to race around and grab the bull by the tail and pull him over.'

'Pull him over?'

'Hmm,' he said, applying a match to his cigarette. 'Once they're buggered, they pull over easy. I just tie 'em up and winch 'em onto the truck.'

'What do you do with them then?' I asked.

'Oh, sell 'em to the stations. They pick out the best ones for breeding. They just sell off the rest.'

'Where do you do most of your work, Jamie?' I asked him.

'Around Charters Towers; all over the place.'

'Does the work keep you busy all year?'

'Nah,' he replied, disgustedly, 'I can only work about three months of the year.'

'What do you do with the rest of your time?'

'Get pissed!' His reply came quickly and was probably true. As we sat and talked, Moa came in and sat down on the settee beside us. He looked at Jamie and then nodded to me.

'Have you ever seen a piebald crab?' he asked. I looked at him, not knowing what prank he was about to embark on.

'No,' I answered, non-committally, 'what is a piebald crab?' Moa burst out laughing as he slapped Jamie on the shoulder.

'This fella here,' Moa laughed, 'I showed him a lobster before and he reckoned it was the first piebald crab he'd ever seen.' A quick flash of anger crossed Jamie's face but disappeared just as quickly. That twisted smile broke over his face as he looked at us.

'It's alright for you bastards,' he said, good-naturedly, 'you live here. I've hardly seen the sea before. How am I supposed to know it's a lobster. I've never seen one before.'

That night Henry brought a freshly cooked lobster into the kitchen, and tossed it onto the table.

'Get into that,' he invited. 'That's Jamie's piebald crab.' What a succulent feast it proved to be.

We had just finished off the last of the lobster when Assam arrived home. He didn't mind that we had cleaned it all up; he could simply go out and catch another lobster anytime he so desired.

Assam was a sort of 'chucker out' at the local pub, which was rather ridiculous really, because he wasn't a big man. He stood about 155 centimetres (5 feet 2 inches) in his socks and weighed no more than 57 kilograms (about 9 stone). Some of the big blacks who drank at the pub could have blown him away; there were even some really big blacks of about 127 kilograms (20 stone) who could have flicked him away with their fingers. But Assam was respected by the mob and if he went up to some drunken, or just rowdy, blacks and told them to 'piss off' because they were a 'bloody nuisance', they simply went — amid moans of protest, of course. Still, the title of 'chucker out' was certainly a misnomer.

'Where's Moa?' Henry asked him. 'You went out together.'

'Ah, I left him there,' Assam replied. 'I came home to get some sleep. Nobody can sleep with his big mouth.' He smiled as he settled himself on the settee. I'm not sure what he meant by 'big mouth'. Whether he was suggesting that Moa talked too much or that he snored, I cannot say. However, I *can* say that Moa has a very loud voice!

We were sitting around the kitchen table, just talking away, when Henry began to laugh uncontrollably.

'What's up?' Assam asked. 'You gone off, or something?'

'I was just thinking of those white tourists that came over the other day,' he explained. 'Remember, that mob from the bush?'

'Yair. What about them?'

'You remember, we had all those turtle shells hanging around the room and they wanted to know why we "hung all those rocks up". ' Assam burst out laughing, as we all did when we understood what Henry was talking about.

'Yes, I remember,' Assam said. 'They were a funny mob.'

'Didn't they know they were turtle shells?' I asked.

'No, they had no idea,' Henry replied. 'They thought they were big rocks hanging up there.' Henry suddenly convulsed with laughter again. 'They wanted to know if hanging up rocks was part of our Aboriginal culture.' We all laughed at Henry's story.

I looked up at the clock on the wall. It was 11.30 pm. I pointed this out to my friends and told them it was time for me to flake out; I was tired.

In a couple of days I would have to return to Brisbane to check on my mother. I had left her in the Blue Nurses' Nazarene Nursing Home at Redcliffe for the few days I had expected to be away on Palm Island. I had been concerned about her for quite some weeks now because she was off her food. I had taken her to the doctor and he told her that if she didn't get stuck into her tucker he would put her in hospital for a few days to have a bronchoscopy.

I called at Rick's office the following day to let him know I'd be going. I mentioned the newsletter to him and he beamed at the thought of it.

I was just as anxious as he was to get the newsletter into circulation to try to quell this ridiculous faction fighting that was taking place behind the scenes. I was itching to write articles for the people: I was keen to get the problems out into the open where they could be resolved. I felt it was useless and stupid to have one group of blacks huddling in one group, casting sideways glances at another huddle of blacks. Neither group had a clue what was bugging the other side; even if they did know, nothing constructive could be done until both groups sat down to discuss their differences. Some were going to get their noses out of joint, but stiff bikkies! Majority rule, that's the caper.

As I understood it, the main problem was the proposed tourist resort, with one faction wanting it, and the other abhorring it. It seemed to me that if the people could successfully run a tourist business on the island they could turn the tables on the whites. The exploitation would go the other way! Rick, however, didn't see it in that light. 'Palm Island is for Palm Islanders' was his motto. That's fair enough, I suppose, but to use the words of Bill Congoo and others, things were moving too fast for the people.

'Rick,' I asked, 'about this newsletter, what format did you have in mind? How many pages do you envisage?' He placed his hands across his forehead and looked at me.

'Well,' he replied, 'even if we could get one page out it would be a help.'

'Jesus Christ!' I replied. 'What can you say on one piece of paper? It would take almost a page to introduce the bloody thing.'

'What do you reckon?' He looked at me helplessly. 'How big do you reckon it ought to be?' I had had the mistaken idea that he had already planned all these details. I had no idea what he had in mind. Also, I had no idea as to the number of copies he wanted printed or how he was going to print them: photocopy? Gestetner? Did he intend to charge the readers for them? If so, how much? But Rick had no ideas or plans at all. All he wanted was a 'newsletter to unite the people'.

After discussing the matter further with him I was still no wiser. I told him again that I must return to Brisbane the next day. It occurred to me that I might be able to fashion a few copies while I was in Brisbane and take advantage of the more modern facilities there. I could then bring the copies back with me to obtain Rick's approval or disapproval.

'Well, I'm buggered if I know how many pages you want,' I replied. 'Nor do I know how many copies you want. I thought you would have that all worked out.'

'You got any idea?'

'I suppose it depends on how much funding you have,' I said. 'What finance do you have?' He pushed my question aside with a flourish of his hand.

'Oh, there's plenty of funding,' he replied, repeating what he had told me before. 'There's provision in the DCS [Department of Community Services] for a newsletter.'

'Fine,' I replied. 'But how much?'

'I'm not sure. I'll have to find out.' I fully expected he'd know that already. I was very tempted to ask him if I was moving too fast for him. I mean, here was a guy with an idea but with no suggestions on how to implement it. He simply wanted to leave everything to me.

After a few more minutes I left, telling Rick that I would catch up with him on my return from Brisbane. Then I went to the tearoom again and made myself a good, strong cup of coffee. As I stood there, a man of small, wispy build whom I had met some days earlier came up and spoke to me. He was a friendly sort of bloke who seemed to be always smiling. After studying him for a moment or two, I could see why; he had a misshapen top lip and it was this that caused the perpetual smile. He seemed a bit unsettled as he spoke to me.

'Nearly got bit down there before,' he said, pointing towards the calm seas. 'Bloody bastard of a thing nearly got me.' He studied his hand closely.

'What nearly got you?' I asked. 'A shark?'

'No,' he replied. 'There's no way a shark would get me unless it grew legs!'

'Well, what nearly got you, then?' I asked again.

'One of those bloody octopuses,' he said, staring down at the waterfront.

'Look out,' I chided him. 'There are no octopuses down there. The water is too shallow.'

'Come on, then,' he offered, flicking a thumb towards the water, 'I'll show you the little bastards!'

We walked down to where a pool of water had been left by the ebbing tide. He bent down and picked up a piece of stick from the sand. He prodded around in the shallow pool for a while, his eyes wide and searching. Suddenly he jumped back with such rapidity that he frightened the life out of me.

'What?' I exclaimed. For reply, he hooked something like a piece of seaweed out of the pond and held it aloft.

'There,' he said, jubilantly. 'See 'im?'

'No,' I answered, my eyes glued to what he held. 'See bloody what?'

He flung the stick and the object further up the beach and walked around it in a circle.

'There, one of those blue-ringed octopuses.' He flicked it towards me. I jumped back quickly, just in case. I had read reports of these blue-ringed things. According to reports, they are supposed to make you ill if you even look at them! I bent closer as he scratched the sand from around the blab and, sure enough, a blue-ringed octopus was hanging off the end of the stick.

'You watch,' he invited. 'You watch him change colour.' He was right. Soon, vivid blue rings appeared around its body.

'So, that's what they look like,' I mused. 'Wouldn't think a little thing like that could kill you, eh?' It was only about the size of a fifty cent piece.

'Three minutes,' he said, dramatically. 'Three minutes and you're as dead as mutton!' Not being anxious to be turned into a lump of dead mutton, I suggested we skewer it and toss it onto the nearest fire.

'You carry it,' he said, holding the stick out at its full length.

'OK,' I said. I smiled at his genuine fear as I took the stick from him. Smoke was issuing from a 44-gallon drum at the back of the pub, probably where the beer cartons were being burnt. So I headed for it, holding the sand-covered mollusc well out in front of me. Being the mischievous bloke I am, I would dearly have loved to toss the thing at his feet. He would have broken the world record for the high jump; but then again, I might have killed the poor bugger.

'You going back for a paddle?' I asked him, tongue-in-cheek.

'No way!' he replied, drawing a quick breath. 'Some poor bugger is going to get killed with one of those things yet — you see!' He looked across at the open doors of the pub and licked his lips longingly.

'You want a beer?' he asked me.

'Aw, no thanks,' I refused. He dragged his eyes away from the pub and changed direction.

'I don't either,' he said stoically. 'Frig the grog.'

'How long have you been here?' I asked, as we strolled off back to the beach. He stopped and calculated the years on his fingers: for each set of ten fingers he made a mark in the sand until four marks had appeared.

'About forty years,' he replied. 'Might be a bit longer, I dunno.'

'You must have been pretty young when you came here,' I observed.

'About eight,' he replied. 'I was sent here with my old dad. He was sent here for punishment and we all came too.'

'Punishment?' I looked at him. 'Do you know what for?' He squinted his eyes, and for a while I thought he wasn't going to answer my question.

'Aw,' he said, at last, 'my old man nearly killed someone out on a station once. He knocked down some white fella and took to him with a waddy. I don't remember much. It was a long time ago.'

During my visits to some of the far country towns, I had quite often spoken with Aborigines who told me of violence on cattle stations. Some of the things I have been told would make your hair curl: I was told about blacks being belted with stirrup irons, flogged with chains and thrashed with stockwhips; of being bashed for little or no reason and set upon by the whole gang of station workers. I wondered if this man's story might be similar.

'What happened?' I tested. He spat on the ground and looked at me, his misshapen lip hanging limp.

'Ah, well,' he began, 'we were out working one day. We were putting up a fence, I think. Anyway, this fella — this white fella — got mad at my father for something. I don't know what it was. So he up with some barbed wire and belted into my father. The bastard hooked me in the face too.' He held his face upwards at me. 'See my lip? That bastard done that. My father was nearly torn to pieces. My father hit this white fella with a post-hole shovel and knocked him down and started to belt into him with the shovel. Some of his mates raced over and stopped my father; he would've killed him, I reckon.' He stopped talking and shrugged. 'And see,' he continued, 'that barbed wire hooked my father's eye nearly out. He tried to shove it back in but there was all this dirt on his hands, see — from fencin'.' He looked at me.

'You got a smoke?' he asked.

'Yair,' I answered, taking out my packet of cigarettes; I offered him one and took one myself.

'Anyway, my father's got a real bad temper.' He lit both our smokes. 'Real bad temper,' he repeated. He stopped speaking for a while and blew out a blue cloud of smoke. 'Anyway,' he continued, 'when these other blokes came over, my father picked up a crowbar — you know what a crowbar is — and he was going to spear the fella on the ground. He was out cold and my father *would* have speared him, too, if the other white fellas hadn't raced over and belted my father to the ground. He got his eye back in but he couldn't see out of it any more.' He clenched his teeth hard at the memory. I tried to imagine what the scene must have been like: yells, screams, grunts, obscenities.

'You know what?' he was speaking again. 'The bastard was going to tie my father up with barbed wire. That's when I bought into it. I raced in with a stick to try to hit him, but he took to me then.'

He lifted his shirt up around his shoulders to reveal several long raised scars. I caught my breath at the sight. Each was about half an inch across and ran down the length of his back, ending at his hip. What agony he must have suffered!

(Let me digress a little: it is a fact that, when one sees the result of so much cruelty and injury, as I have, one more or less becomes not only hardened to the terrible sights but sick of them as well. Take this present case for example: here is a blackfellow — who can't read or write, through no fault of his own, and whose skin has been ripped to shreds when he was a young boy — all this for trying to stop his father from being bound with barbed wire. What solace is there for the thousands of elderly Aborigines whose bones are misshapen because they were broken in the white man's pursuit of profit? Instead of proper treatment, bones of the legs and arms were allowed to heal into the most hideous and grotesque shapes. Now here I was gazing at the back of this blackfellow whose skin had been mercilessly and deliberately ripped with barbed wire. Where, I wondered, had it all ended in those early days?)

'And it was because of this incident that your father was sent to Palm Island?'

'Hey?' He didn't understand my question.

'Was your dad sent to Palm Island because of this fight?'

'Aw, yes. That was it alright. We was all sent over here.'

'What was it like when you first came here?' I asked. 'Like it is now?'

He looked at me sharply and shook his head vigorously.

'Shit, no,' he replied quickly. 'There was none of these houses when we come here.' He spread his hands as he gestured towards the village. 'We had to make our own house. Only grass houses in those days.'

'How did you make them?' I enquired.

'Oh, we pulled out the long grass and plaited it up,' he explained. 'They were good, but they leaked a bit when it rained. They were warm though.'

'Did you have plenty to eat?' I asked. 'You know, did they feed you?' He smiled tolerantly at my question.

'They fed us a bit,' he replied, 'but it was a sort of a ration. We got about a spoonful of tea and sugar, and a bit of corned meat and a bit of bread. That's all they gave us.'

'What about butter?' I asked him. He thought for a while before answering.

'Aw, yes, we got a bit of butter. We used to get a bit of syrup too. We used to mix the butter and syrup together and make a sort of paste and put it on our bread. It wasn't too bad either.' He laughed softly to himself. As he opened his mouth I noticed for the first time that his teeth were perfectly formed and as white as teeth could be. I remarked on this.

'Aw, I don't know,' he said modestly. 'I used to peel coconuts with my teeth. White people have told me that's why they're so good.'

'Peel coconuts?' I asked.

'Yes. You know, with my teeth. A lot of people used a steel point to rip the husk off but I did it with my teeth.' He looked up towards the football field and noticed some coconuts lying on the ground beneath some coconut trees. He began to walk slowly up the slight gradient towards them.

'Come,' he invited, 'I'll show you how it's done.' In no time we were there and he had picked up one of the coconuts. The husk was hard, the coconut having only recently fallen from the tree. Several people gathered around, obviously aware of what was about to take place, and were soon joined by about a dozen kids whose bush telegraph was working perfectly. Without further ado, our entertainer sunk his teeth into the tough husk and with a quick, hard twist pulled the coconut away from his mouth. Off came a strip of husk the full length of the coconut. He repeated the move, and a second large strip of the tough fibre came loose. After about six or seven similar moves the nut had been completely stripped of its husk. The onlookers soon drifted away, except for the dozen or so kids who were trying desperately to duplicate the feat. One smart kid, though, wasn't the least bit interested in trying out his teeth: he casually walked over, picked up the clean nut and took off! Some of the other kids saw him but they were too late; soon he was safely home.

I congratulated my friend. Shrugging his shoulders, he then walked back down towards the pub. I was at a loose end, so I too wandered down to the pub. As I entered, the television set was blaring out loudly, though no one appeared to be watching it. Opposite the television set two young men were earnestly engaged in a game of pool, their eyes rolling just about as much as the pool balls they were trying to pocket. Each shot — or more correctly miscue — was followed by peals of laughter. The place was pretty dark and it was difficult to recognise those who were sitting around the alcove tables drinking their beer. As I neared the tables, however, a hand came out and clutched at me. It was Tom, one of the people who had turned up for old Assam's washed-out birthday barbecue.

'Come an' 'ave a drink, Bill,' he said. He seemed to be fairly sober for that time of day so I dragged up a chair, wiped some spilled beer off the table, and sat down. There was a large jug of beer on the table in front of him and he invited me to share it. I poured some of the amber liquid into a used glass and started to drink it. I almost gagged.

He laughed softly at my discomfort.

'What the fucking hell is this?' I asked, holding the glass up to the light. He laughed gently again.

'There's a little bit of white lady in it,' he confessed.

'White lady?'

'Metho,' he said, matter-of-factly. 'There's only a little bit in it. It'll put a sparkle in you.' Well, I really didn't need a sparkle of that nature.

'How long are you stayin', Bill?' he enquired. 'Haven't seen you for a while.'

'Oh, only for a little while,' I replied. 'I just want to see what's around to write about.' I told him of the plan to print a newsletter for the people on the island.

He welcomed the idea. 'If there's anything I can do, Bill, just let me know,' he offered.

'Well,' I asked him, 'do you know of anything interesting I could write about? You know, maybe some early history of the island.' He wiped a hairy arm across his mouth as he thought for a moment. Then he looked at me suddenly.

'How about those old planes up in the bush?' he asked. 'You seen 'em?'

'No,' I replied. 'What planes?' He sipped his beer and peered at me over the top of his glass.

'Oh, there's some seaplanes up in the bush,' he informed me. 'Those Yanks brought them here during the war.' As he finished speaking his eyes seemed to blaze in anger. 'The bastards!' he spat out.

'Why do you call them bastards?' I asked him.

He was so angry at the thought of those Yanks that he fumbled for words. He glowered at me.

'Those fuckin' bastards!' he managed to blurt out. 'They rooted all our women here.' I got the feeling that his wife might have been one of the women! I was unsure as to whether I should proceed with this conversation, but, throwing caution (and good sense) to the winds, I decided to press on.

'I'm sorry about that,' I offered, cautiously, 'but you seem to know about those old aircraft up there in the bush. And you did offer to help. What do you know about them? Did they crash?'

'No, I don't think so,' he replied quietly. He had settled down so quickly that he surprised me. Perhaps it was the sparkle of the white lady.

'See,' he continued, 'during the war the Yanks had some sort of base here. They had planes and buildings and machine-guns set into big concrete blocks. It was a big thing with them.' He grunted in disgust and spat out the doorway. 'Well, you know the Yanks,' he continued, scornfully. 'They do things in a big way.' He stretched out the 'big'. 'When they left they just left it all here, planes and all.'

A drinker at a table next to ours leaned over to us. He had been listening to our conversation and now felt compelled to interrupt.

'Still think that plane crashed,' he remarked. A vacuous expression covered his face as he looked at us.

'Aw, shut up and drink your fuckin' beer, Marty,' my friend reproved him. 'You wouldn't know what fuckin' day it was!'

The intruder leaned back hurriedly into his chair, making a rude movement with his forefinger. We ignored him and he settled back, sipping his beer.

'No, see,' Tom spoke again, 'what happened was, they had a few of these seaplanes here. When they left, they didn't take this one — I'm sure there was more than one. It wouldn't fly, or something.'

'How did they get them here?' I realised how stupid the question was even before I had finished asking it. Of course, they were aeroplanes, and aeroplanes *flew*.

'They were flown here,' was his obvious reply. 'They used to fix them up here. They used to make so much fuckin' noise. They'd come in low over the houses — they were only little huts then, in those days. They used to come in and skim along the water until they stopped. I used to like watching them.' He drank a large draft of his beer before continuing. 'The kids used to swim out to them when they were floating on the water but the Yanks used to chase them. They fired a gun a few times but not to shoot them, just to scare them away.' The beer jug was empty and I brought it to his attention.

'Want to fill it up again?' I asked him as I rose from the table.

'Aw, yes,' he replied. 'Might as well, eh? Bloody oath.'

'OK,' I answered. 'But none of that white bitch this time, eh?'

He lowered his head and smiled to himself. 'Alright,' he conceded, 'but it'll be hard to take.'

I had the jug refilled and brought it back to the table. 'You mentioned something about machine-gun emplacements,' I said to him. 'What were they used for?'

'In case the Japs came, I suppose,' he replied. 'Jesus Christ! They had bloody guns everywhere.'

The old joker who had interrupted our conversation earlier rose and came around to our table. 'Those Japs nearly got us too,' he remarked, his voice slightly more slurred than previously.

'You're not 'ere again, are you?' my companion said to him. 'Piss off!'

The interloper returned to his table but not before he had quickly filled his glass from my jug of beer. Cunning old bastard!

'I'll have to go and have a look at those aeroplanes,' I said to him.

'When you going?' he asked.

'Well, I'd like to go tomorrow but I'll have to make a phone call to Brisbane first.' If when I rang the nursing home they told me my mother was OK, I'd put off going to the city until the following day.

'If you don't go too early,' he offered, 'I'll go with you.' That suited me fine. I'd have a ready-made guide to take me to the spot in the bush where the aircraft was.

'How about 11 o'clock?' I asked.

'That would be alright,' he agreed.

'OK,' I replied. 'I'll go and make my phone call and be right back to let you know for sure if I can go tomorrow.'

I went across to the telephone box and placed my call; I got through almost immediately and found that my mother's condition was good enough for me to put off my journey for a day. I hurried back to the pub to tell my friend.

'That'll be good,' he said. 'We can meet here at the pub at about half past ten.' I smiled at his proposition: he wanted to come with me but he wasn't going to miss out on his couple of beers first.

Chapter 8

When we entered the pub the following day, it was already busy, with jugs being filled with beer. Thankfully, though, it wasn't too long before we were on our way to the outskirts of the village and onwards towards the mystery of the flying boats. As we passed Tom's house — one of the last in the village — Tom picked up two vicious-looking spears that were leaning against the fence.

'We pass through a good fishing spot,' he explained. 'Might spear a feed on the way back. The tide should be up by then.' He tossed the spears over his shoulder and we proceeded on our way. The going was pretty rugged because, although the bush had been cleared some years ago, the new growth was thick and strong. As we passed a small inlet, my companion pointed to a spot on the edge of the opposite bank and slowed his pace.

'There was a big murder done there once,' he informed me. 'It was a bloody awful thing.' I pricked up my ears, sensing that I was about to hear of some ghastly event of past days. I looked at him, frowning in a manner that was almost overkill as far as a silent question was concerned.

'A couple of kids were playing out there one day and they found a boat floating loose,' he explained. 'The kids went over to the boat and found a dead body in it.' He looked at me with wide eyes. 'Anyway,' he continued, 'they came pelting back to the town and told the people there. The police were called and a big mob of people went out to see what was going on.' He peered across to where the boat had been found all those years ago, as if expecting to see it. 'When the police looked at the body they didn't know who it was; none of the people had ever seen him before.'

'Was he a black man or a white man?' I asked.

'He was a blackfella,' Tom replied. 'After a while everybody all went home and the police went back for a truck to take the body back. And you know what?' — he spoke barely above a whisper — 'When they came back there was nothing to be seen. No boat, no body, nothing!' I lit a smoke. I must admit Tom's manner scared me a bit.

Obviously, *he* was scared and somehow his feelings were being passed on to me. It's my nature that when I'm out in a strange and uninhabited bush and someone tells me about dead bodies my neck hair creeps and my eyes tend to move around.

'Did they find it — the body?' I asked nervously.

'Never ever found nothing,' he answered. 'Nobody knows what happened. A lot of people — just about everybody — reckon it was the Kadaitcha. They reckon he was there to get payback. They used to do that, you know.'

'Hang on,' I objected. 'How could a boat and a body just disappear?' He gave me a 'what sort of a dickhead are you' look, but made no reply.

'We better get going,' he suggested, as he leaned his spears against a bush. 'I'll leave these here until we come back. No sense taking them through the bush.'

'They might disappear!' I couldn't help making the jibe.

He remained silent. But he wasted no time in getting away from this spooky area, and I was only slightly behind him!

After thrashing our way through the thick underbrush for about half an hour, we came into a clearing. On the other side of it, under a covering of shrubbery, I could make out the contour of a Catalina flying boat. I walked into the huge interior of the abandoned aircraft but there was very little to see; certainly nothing that could be taken as a souvenir. Nothing but the shell remained.

'Well, I've seen enough,' I said to Tom. 'Why don't we go and spear a fish?' Of course, by 'we' I meant 'him'. There'd be no way in the world that I would be going into the sea to any depth above my ankles! Years before, on Bribie Island, I had had one terrifying experience with sharks and one is enough!

Tom made no response but muttered as we walked across to some bushes and pulled them aside.

'This is where they had one of those machine-guns,' he told me. 'There used to be a lot of them around here but I can't see any more.'

'Probably rusted away,' I suggested. 'It must be a long time since they were put here.' He nodded his head in agreement.

'I suppose so,' he remarked, 'but it wouldn't surprise me if those bloody kids ripped them off.' I looked at the unimpressive mass of rusted metal for a few moments.

'How's that tide?' I urged him. 'There must be millions of fish swimming around out there by now.'

He gave a sardonic grin but said nothing. He let the bushes fall back into place and we headed back into the bush once more. As we reached the place where he had left his spears — where the boat and the body had disappeared — he didn't stop, but clutched his spears up as he walked quickly by. He didn't even look at the inlet. I imagined he might be fearful of seeing the Kadaitcha which to him was some strange being capable of terrifying and vengeful transmogrification. Nevertheless, I somehow took the lead, and in a very short while we had opened up a considerable distance between us and that spooky place. As we walked along the beach towards the township, he turned off abruptly to his right and paddled into the water until it was up to his waist.

'You're bloody mad!' I called out to him. 'A shark will grab you.' He turned towards me and sneered. He walked slowly around and then remained perfectly still, his cruel five-pronged spear poised slightly above the water. I watched him, his eyes following the fish as it moved through the water. Suddenly he uncoiled like some giant spring: the spear drove down into the water and he gave it a final thrust. When the spear cleared the water again, a huge fish was impaled on its prongs. It thrashed helplessly as he waded back to the beach. Grinning broadly, he held it aloft.

'You beauty!' I exclaimed. 'What a ripper! What is it?'

'Ah, we call it "white fish",' he replied. 'Another name for it is "trevally". Very nice fish, eh?'

It certainly was a nice fish. It was about three feet long and as thick as my thigh. As we walked through the village, people turned to admire the day's catch. Some people even wanted to buy it from him.

'Give ya a carton of beer for it, Tommy,' one of them said. Tom laughed at the offer.

'Huh, fuck you!' he said with a good-natured smile.

'Where ya catch 'im?'

'Just up there,' Tom replied, nodding vaguely in the direction from which we had come. Tom was a bit too cunning for them. There was no way he was going to let on where his favourite fishing spot was.

'You come,' he said to me. I was not sure if it was an instruction or an invitation.

I said nothing and followed him back to his small house. He stood his two fishing spears up against the wall of the building and we both entered. Inside, there seemed to be turtle shells everywhere — small ones, huge ones. There were at least eight carapaces: some were hanging on the walls and some just lying on the floor. The odour was almost unbearable. It was obvious that Tom lived alone: the place was a mess. In the yard at the rear of the house several fishing spears were leaning against the wall, all with various shaped prongs. Horses for courses, I thought, as I fingered the wicked-looking barbs. One of the spears was about fifteen feet long. Tom made his way towards an open fireplace, beside which was a large hole with rocks scattered around it.

'We cook this bugger,' Tom said, as he gathered up some of the twigs and dry wood stacked up beside the fireplace. When the fire caught, he placed some of the rocks on top of it. He took the fish down to the beach and cleaned it and by the time he returned the fire was burning briskly and heating the rocks. Tom raked out the stones and most of the glowing coals. He then placed a layer of stones in the bottom of the hole and placed the fish on top of them, placed the remainder of the hot rocks on top and covered them with a few bags, then with sand. In this oven the fish took only about twenty minutes to cook. What a way to cook fish! The white flesh simply fell from the bones. There was too much for us, so Tom called over a few kids who had been playing about on the reef. They sat down and had soon finished off the remainder of the succulent flesh.

'Where you bin get 'im?' one of the kids dared to ask.

'You f'la go now,' Tom said to them, pointing with his chin towards the beach. They rose abruptly, and without any further conversation hurried away. It appeared that when Tom spoke, his words were respected.

'Tom,' I enquired, 'have you lived here all of your life?'

He placed his hand gingerly on one of the rocks and, having ascertained that it was cool enough, eased his backside onto it. I followed suit.

'Ah, no,' he answered. 'No. I don't come from here. I came here when I was a little boy.' He looked out across the sea. Suddenly he appeared to become sad and unhappy, his eyes seeming to be focused on some imaginary object out to sea. I studied him: I had no idea what his age would be — neither did he, I fancy — but I think it would be fair to say that he would never see seventy again. His hair was curly and snowy-white, yet there were wisps of a darker shade. His brow was very heavy and pronounced, with deep furrows creasing his forehead; his eyebrows thick and untidy, like the ends of a well-worn broom. They almost succeeded in hiding his black eyes, in which no pupils could be discerned. The nose flattened out suddenly and his lips were thick and protruding. The rest of his features were almost hidden by a four-day growth of prickly, grey beard. But it was the eyes that captured my attention: sorrow, disappointment. Something was hurting this man.

Should I leave him to his agony or should I talk to him with the hope of giving him some release? I decided on the latter course. The story he told to me will remain in my memory forever — even his way of speaking seemed to change with his emotions.

'It be 'bout three years ago, now,' he began. 'Marnie — that my wife — and me go to Mt Isa for our son. He lived there. He lived with a mate of his. We all get a job on a station for a while.' He looked up at me and there could be no doubt that his eyes were moist. I picked at an imaginary spot on my shirt. I had to have a reason to avoid his eyes.

'We work there for a month of two,' he continued. 'Then we all go back to town for a spell. Too much rain to work.'

'Mt Isa?' I queried.

'Mt Isa,' he nodded. 'We all do a bit of shoppin', you know, for a little while.' He took a deep breath and his gaze returned to the sea. I remained silent.

'Any'ow,' he resumed his story. 'That f'la — my boy's mate — he take us to where he had his house a little bit out of town but there was a big gully there, before we get to his place, and all that rain, you know, it make a lot of water in that gully. Can't cross.' He made a sweeping motion with his hand before continuing.

'My boy and his mate, they cross but it dangerous, you know. My son, he chuck a rope over so my Marnie, my wife, can cross. She grab the rope and the other two pull her over but that rope, it break.' He stood up quickly as if, on seeing the tragic scene again, he wanted to help his wife. A sound came from deep within his throat and ended with a low, blood-curdling gurgle.

'Hey!' I said, as I touched the old man lightly on the shoulder. 'No more. It's no good. Don't say any more about it.' He gently pulled his shoulder from my light grasp and looked squarely at me once more.

'No worries,' he said, intent on further torturing himself. 'It don't matter. Better I say it.'

'Well, alright, Tom,' I spoke gently to the old man, 'if you think you can handle it.'

'Handle? What handle?' I explained the context of my statement in modern-day parlance. He assured me that telling me would not unduly upset him.

'Marnie, she get washed down the gully. We all raced down and she was caught in a log. Her head go down and come up; go down and come up again. Nothing we could do. Then my son, he jump in.'

He winced again as the memory and the mental pictures sprang into his mind.

'They both drown,' he said, bluntly. 'I see Marnie, the water running over her face.' He uttered that terrible agonised cry again, more deep-throated than before. 'My boy, he gone; we never find him.'

'I better leave soon.' Tom had returned to the present: 'Maybe find another woman. Then I might go back out to the bush.' He had brightened up a bit at the thought of the bush.

'Where would you go?' I asked, hoping to erase the memory that tortured his mind, at least temporarily.

'Don't know.' He pursed his lips at my question. 'Might go to Winton. Plenty friend there.' He laughed lightly for a moment. 'But hard. Hard Palm Island. Long time.' His voice trailed off.

Now that Tom had regained his composure, some of the folds seemed to have disappeared from his forehead.

'Tom,' I asked. 'Did you go to school here, on Palm Island?'

'Oh yes,' he replied. 'But not long. I work. I go to work. They work us pretty young, them days.'

'What sort of work, Tom?'

'Wood. I carry wood.' He gave a quick twist of his head to emphasise his words. 'Hard work.'

'Carry wood?' I queried. 'Where did you carry it to?'

'Houses,' he replied. 'I used to carry it to the houses. No 'lectricity, them days. All wood stoves.'

'But there wouldn't have been many houses here in those days, would there?'

'Only white f'la,' he answered. 'Not many.'

'What was your house like? Was it a grass one?'

'Hey, look out,' he laughed. 'No house; only big shed.' Tom then explained to me that the young men and boys lived in dormitories where they were treated pretty strictly. I asked him about the food.

'Not good tucker,' he told me. 'Salty pork, salt beef, bread — that sort of thing. Alright, I suppose. We get hungry, we eat anything.'

'Your father dead now?' I asked. What an absolutely stupid bloody question! I reproved myself. Here was an old man, maybe pushing eighty, and I ask him if his father is dead! Fortunately, Tom didn't see it that way.

'Yes, he dead a long time,' he answered. 'He get killed up there.' As he spoke, he pointed with a limp hand towards the mountains to the east of the island. I pricked my ears with interest.

'How?' I asked, without quite realising how indecently, and indelicately, I had asked the question. 'I mean,' I tried to recover, 'what happened to him?' Tom shrugged one shoulder.

'Tree,' he answered. 'A tree fall on him. Squash him.'

I looked away from him quickly. When one asks questions of this nature, one can never be sure how literal the answer is going to be, or how sensitive the subject might become. In this case, the answer had been a bit too pithy for me: Tom's face was quite contorted and I decided not to press on with this line of questioning.

'Too bad,' Tom said, before I had a chance to change the subject. 'Shouldn't have happened. He was in the bush having a shit when the silly bastards fall a tree on him. They must have known he was there.'

He shook his head sadly, but now that he had elected to keep the subject going, I decided to see it through.

'How about your mother?' I enquired. 'How did she, er, pass on?' 'Eh?'

How does one ask these sorts of questions in a delicate manner? 'How did your mother die?' He twisted his lips matter-of-factly before replying.

'She get that Pamony,' he told me. I thought for a while.

'Pneumonia?'

'Yes, that one,' he answered.

Now it was time to change tack. 'Have you always worked on your wood job or did you do some other kind of work too?' He turned a stiff neck towards me, his eyes narrowed and his nose wrinkling.

'Nah,' he replied. 'I used to empty them white fellas' shit tins too. I had to dig trenches for it.'

'When you first came to Palm Island, how did you live?'

'Up to shit!' He smiled at his choice of words. Now that we had finished with his painful earlier memories, Tom seemed to be more himself. 'We were all put in a big dormitory. I don't remember how many of us were locked up in there. They only let us out to work. When we were locked up, there was nothing to do and a lot of fights broke out. I can remember kids rolling around on the floor, fighting. There was no floor, really; it was just dirt, stamped down hard and some sort of white powder on it. That white stuff stung our feet. When a kid got some skin knocked off by fighting, that white stuff used to get in and sting like fucking hell.' Tom rubbed his elbow as if he were feeling some phantom pain from the past. 'It used to be a bastard when it rained,' he continued. 'The water used to run in and make the ground into mud. That was when it hurt our feet most.'

'What was that white stuff?'

'It was something they reckon killed the bed bugs and lice — you know, that sort of thing. I don't know what it was called but, by Christ, it used to burn us.'

'Sounds like it might have been lime,' I suggested.

'Whatever it was,' Tom said, sarcastically, 'it didn't stop the fucking bed bugs!'

'Did you ever complain about it?'

'No good,' he answered, with a sneer. 'All that would happen was that you'd get a belt across the ear and told to shut up. At times, if we whinged too much, the whole mob of us would get into trouble. It wouldn't matter what time of night it was, we'd all have to get out of bed and we were given a log or a rock to hold between our legs and made to walk around in a circle. Some of us would fall arse-over-head and sometimes a log or a rock would catch our fingers on the ground. They split open sometimes.'

'That would be painful,' I remarked.

'Painful,' he scowled. 'Specially if you got that white stuff in the split.' He stopped talking and sat deep in thought for a while, no doubt remembering those days of hell.

'It was a bastard in the winter time,' he continued. 'We were freezing cold and we'd get big cracks in our fingers and in our feet.' He rummaged around in his coat pocket and drew out a crumpled packet of tobacco. I had been unaware until then that he smoked. He rolled a thin cigarette and handed the packet to me. I accepted it and rolled myself a skinny smoke.

'Another trick the bastards used to get up to was make us run around in a ring. If we didn't run fast enough, they used to belt us on the ankles with a waddy. Some of the kids' ankles were black and blue. They could hardly walk.'

This wasn't the first time I had heard about this type of treatment of black kids. Fred Clay had told me similar stories of receiving this barbaric treatment when he was a kid in the dormitory.

'See,' Tom was speaking again, 'all us kids belonged to different tribes and we all had our own cultures and customs. A lot of us couldn't understand what each of us was talking about a lot of times; we had different lingoes. But those white fellas couldn't understand that. They thought that because we were all black we must all talk the same. They fucking stupid, those fellas.' He threw back his head in amusement. 'There were kids from Charleville, Boulia, Winton — all over,' he resumed. 'They all talk in a different way. Not all the same. Different habits too.'

'Didn't you kids have any time to yourselves — you know, to play or something?'

'No.' He spat the word out. 'Work! That's all we do. We keep the whole place clean, then we have to go and clean up the jail block.' Tom gave an involuntary choke as he recalled his childhood. 'Those cells used to make us sick. Some of them were in jail for getting drunk on some stuff they used to make out of wild plum, so you can think what the place was like. They spew everywhere. Not only that, some of them used to shit all over the place, too, and we had to clean it up with a mop and a kerosene tin.' He pulled out an old rag from his pocket and wiped his face with it. The rag was pretty dirty and I wondered silently if his face had been cleaner before he wiped it. I think he used that old rag for everything; there were even a few blood stains on it. Before he replaced it in his pocket he held it to his nose and blew. I turned away so he wouldn't see my lips tighten as I tried to control my gag. A weird, tinny taste affected my mouth.

'Ah, I think I'll see if I can't get a drink somewhere,' he said, as he dragged on the last of his cigarette.

'Yair, right-o,' I replied, rising from my hard rock. 'I'll see you later.'

I walked up towards the shop and sat on the retaining wall. Almost as soon as I was seated, a voice greeted me.

'Well, fancy seeing you here.' It was Mary Twaddle: she'd been a member of the Aboriginal Council when Fred Clay was Chairman.

'Hello, Mary,' I greeted her. 'You're looking well. As a matter of fact,' I flattered her, 'you look younger'. She was a tall woman, with hair now streaked with grey, and a few more lines on her face than when I had last seen her. But her figure hadn't changed, and her hips and shoulders were firmly set. We talked about old times for a few moments, and then her happy expression changed to one of sadness.

'It's a shame about Iris, isn't it?' she remarked.

'Yes,' I replied with equal sadness. 'She was a real fighter, wasn't she?' Mary nodded slowly.

We sat for a while thinking of Iris Clay. I thought of how sick she had been when I saw her in Charters Towers, and of the fierce way she had fought for Aboriginal rights. I remembered her saying to me one day, 'Bill, if I thought screaming would help, I would scream all day'.

Mary and I yarned on for quite some time.

'Well, Bill,' she said, at last. 'I suppose I had better be getting home. They'll all be yelling out for a feed soon and I'll have to go and get some bread.' She rose, gave me a wave, and walked down and entered the shop.

I had promised to call in and have a drink with one or two of the blokes, so I strolled up towards the pub. I didn't really want a drink. Maybe, I thought, hopefully, they'd be well and truly pissed by now and I wouldn't have to have one.

As I got closer to the pub I saw one of them engaged in a 'life-or-death' struggle with a couple of women. They had the poor old codger down on the ground and were shouting and yelling. Of course, he wasn't getting hurt: he was covering himself up too well for that to happen. I doubt if a black snake could have penetrated his defensive smother.

'You wormy bastard,' one of the women was shouting, 'you drink everything you see.' As she finished her tirade she let go with an uppercut through a small gap he had carelessly left unprotected for a moment. The blow snapped his head back with a sickening jolt. But the old joker was now spurred into action: he uncurled himself and sprang to his feet with surprising agility.

'Ya rotten old bitch,' he roared, 'I'll smash ya.' The women attackers were somewhat taken aback by this sudden new twist. They threw their arms into the air and fled, intimidated by the rage of the old man. The women bordered on the obese, so their exit from the fight scene wasn't all that fast and, drunk as he was, he had no trouble in overtaking them. He lifted one foot and booted the closest lady fair in the backside. How he managed to accomplish this without falling arse-over-head I'll never know. She let out a scream of alarm and dived off at a tangent, leaving the other fat bottom within easy sight. He caught the other woman flush behind the ear and her hand flew up to her head to protect herself from further thumps. She escaped through a back yard and hurtled through a door, slamming it resoundingly behind her. Her pursuer was in a terrible fury, but he gave up the chase, satisfied with his victory, and returned once more to the pub where he turned his attention to the amber fluid. I decided against going into the pub and, camouflaging myself as well as I could, I walked quickly past and kept going. Soon I was out of sight around the bend in the road and heading for my place of abode.

When I reached the house, I found several friends from my previous visit to the island talking about the value of possums as tucker; one of them suggested that we go and shoot a couple. This idea brought back memories of my last possum hunt, back in 1974.

There were four of us on that occasion: Fred Clay, Dennis Walker, Don Brady and myself. We drove up the mountain in Fred's four-wheel-drive vehicle, each of us hanging on to a door handle. How we were supposed to shoot anything from that position I don't know because one hand held the door handle and the other grasped the rifle. But we also needed a hand to hold the torch, an essential item on such a safari. When we realised the impossible positions we had taken up, we almost fell off the vehicle with laughter. So Fred stopped and we organised ourselves a bit better. It was decided that Don would walk on ahead, scouring the treetops with the beam of the torch, and we would follow slowly behind in the vehicle, potting possums the light might reveal. This wasn't a good move really; there was nothing wrong with the plan itself, but Don's hand was none too steady — I'll leave the reason for this to the reader's imagination — and the light swooped around everywhere except into the trees.

Dennis was the first to lose his cool.

'Hey, Don,' he yelled at the torchbearer, 'put the light up in the fucking trees, will ya! There ain't no possums on the bloody ground!'

'Aw, righto,' came Don's reply. The beam somehow found its way up into the trees and all eyes stared expectantly among the branches. Fred forgot that he was the driver.

'Fred! Fred, look out!' I realised it was my voice that was screaming in alarm. I looked down and saw that the wheels were just about over the side of the narrow mountain track. Fred gave a grunt and gave the steering wheel a fierce jerk to the right. Well, the vehicle didn't go over the side but Fred's action sent us all flying off the sides and crashing into the undergrowth. Poor Don got such a fright at our screaming and the sudden movement of the vehicle that he fell over the side. He rolled down the mountain for some distance, hanging tenaciously to the torch whose beam first pointed to the sky and then flashed among the trees. Then there was darkness; the torch must have got broken. We listened for sounds of movement in order to find out where our poor old torchbearer was. Nothing! As we looked at each other in mild alarm, the reflection of the headlights turned our faces into waxen images. Suddenly we heard a rustle and a loud breaking of saplings.

'Ah, fuck the possums,' we heard Don say vehemently, then his black round face appeared over the edge of the track, a mask of disgust. He had lost the torch.

'What the fucking hell did you do that for, Fred?' he demanded. 'Jesus Christ! You couldn't drive a shit cart!' In spite of our near calamity the three of us howled with laughter. Not a smile appeared on Don's face.

'Ah, you must be fucking mad,' he accused us, brushing his hand across his face. When he brought it away, he saw blood on it — that really freaked him. He walked over closer to the headlights; his eyes widened.

'Well, I'll be stuffed,' he expostulated. 'I think my face is half torn off and all you silly bastards can do is laugh.' He spat viciously onto the ground. More blood! The look that appeared on Don's face made us howl even louder. Actually, as it turned out, he wasn't badly hurt at all: a few mere scratches and a slightly bitten tongue were the sum total of his wounds. But Don had the capacity to display such a woeful countenance when things went against him.

Dennis eventually found the torch resting against a tree, and after I bumped it against a log it began working again. I don't know how we managed it, but we ended up with five possums that night.

'I'll take 'em home and cook 'em,' Don volunteered. This was fine by us because it was about 3 am and there was no way we were going to stuff around with possums at that hour.

Our adventure had a humorous end, depending on how you look at it, I suppose. You see, when we went down to Don's place later in the day, smacking our lips for a feed of roast possum, we found there was none to eat. The old bugger had fallen asleep when he got home, but not before a passing resident had admired the possums, which Don had heaped on the ground near the fire. Don told him to take them home with him. All we ever got of those possums was their aroma drifting lazily up the valley as they roasted on the fires below. We chided him gently; he smiled sheepishly but said nothing. Don later died in Brisbane of a heart attack. He was, indeed, a good old mate.

Anyway, I joined the suggested possum shoot, and could scarcely keep my eyes open the next day. But I managed to board the small aircraft which was to transport me to Townsville for my journey back to Brisbane.

Chapter 9

When I arrived back in Brisbane, I called at the Redcliffe nursing home where my mother was being cared for. She seemed in good spirits but you could never tell with her: she seldom complained. Her only complaint was that she found it difficult to eat a meal.

I took her home and made her comfortable, then called her doctor in to have a look at her. He was Dr Ho, an Asian, and a very good doctor he had proved to be. He was also my personal doctor, having attended to me now for quite some time. He checked her over thoroughly, then warned her, in his best bedside manner, of course, that if she didn't eat her meals, he would put something horrible down her throat and have a look around down there.

Even this threat couldn't induce her to eat and in the next few weeks she lost about twenty-five kilos. I asked Dr Ho to call again to have another look at her and he arrived shortly after, leaving a few non-urgent patients in his surgery. My mother asked, 'Is he Dr Ho, Dr No or Dr Who?' She still had her sense of humour.

Carlos Ho was as good as his word. He bundled her off to the Redcliffe Hospital to have the promised examination performed. The result of the examination absolutely astounded me: my poor mother was suffering from cancer of the oesophagus and surrounding areas, inoperable.

She was admitted into the Redcliffe Hospital but did not respond at all. I then had her admitted to the Prince Charles Hospital (in Chermside, Brisbane) in order to obtain the second opinion. The sentence was the same: about two months to live. Of course, coward that I am, I didn't tell her the entire story. I fobbed her off by saying it was merely a blockage in her food pipe and that the injections she was receiving would, in time, cure her. There was nothing more the hospital could do for her and they advised me to bring her home. Her doctor could keep the pain at bay.

I brought her home and set up a comfortable bed along a wall in my office. I erected a mirror on my desk in which I could keep my eye on her in case she needed anything. It was really heartbreaking, just sitting there, watching my mother die. But what could I do? I was helpless.

As I watched one day, I noticed that her breathing had become irregular. As I rose from my chair to go to her, she opened her moist, blue eyes.

'How are you going, love?' I asked her. 'Would you like a cold drink?'

There was no reply, and I looked at her more closely. She was dead.

I will never forget how her eyes had opened brightly, immediately before she died. Had she realised she was going? Was it a final, silent goodbye?

Ah, well. Not having any brothers or sisters, here I was alone in the world. As I sat there, gazing down at her serenity, I reflected on the battles we had fought together: the battling for a feed when I was young; and the long walk she had to the farm in Toogoolawah where she had spent hours in the boiling sun, pulling corn. I could see once more the huge sunburn blisters on her back, the sore, cracked hands, and the ready smile she always had for me. And I remembered her reaction to the showman who had propositioned her when I was six.

She was cremated two days later. I didn't have a church service — just a few words by the funeral director's own minister, and then a eulogy I had written in her honour. I am honoured to repeat here the exact words I said:

> I am looking down at my mother's face as she lies, contented, there.
> I see the love within her heart; blue eyes and snow-white hair.
> And, as I watch, her hand in mine, memories come rushing back
> Of the many times she cried for me when I was on the track.
> But I never heard her silent prayers, her tears were shed in vain.
> I never knew, as life rolled on, that I caused her so much pain.
> For I was just a wandering son; I did not know — or care —
> That my mother's heart cried out for me but I was never there.

'Don't forget to keep in touch,' she begged me, through her tears.
I never did and now those words come ringing in my ears.
But it's too late now to say to her, 'I've come back home, to stay.'
I know she has forgiven me for the years I've stayed away.
Praise God; to live life over, no tears would mother vent.
I would devote to those words she wrote but now forever, I shall repent.
Too late! Alas, too late it is for a son to show devotion.
The Grim Reaper's hook has passed her way, now that son must bleed emotion.
As I gaze again at my mother's face, a beauteous sight I see.
With her lips apart, her shining eyes are smiling up at me.
My mother! Oh, my mother, leave me not, I pray.
For my wanton deeds and your loneliness I will many times repay.
Praise God! Praise God, in my selfishness, take another.
For the greatest love of all my life is lying there — my mother.
Let not her eyes grow dim nor her head be bended low.
Let us, once again, relive the past of so long ago.
But if, in Thy wisdom, Thee knowest best, and take her far away.
Tell her that she and her only son will meet again someday.
At last ... all is quiet ... the birds have hushed their song.
And the flowers sigh as they hear me cry ... they know my dear mother has gone.

Then the coffin, over which was draped the Aboriginal flag, was trundled away on the conveyor belt. It soon disappeared behind the curtain, and into the fires of oblivion.

The week following my mother's death I went back to Palm Island. My friends were at a loss as to why I was so subdued on my return. I explained to them about Mum's death and they comforted me. But life goes on, however difficult it may be.

One afternoon, a group of people gathered at Assam's house. The conversation was jolly and carefree, until Rick drove up. He was always a serious one and took his job as Chairman of the Aboriginal

Council very seriously indeed. He began talking to us about the problems the people of Palm Island faced.

'I can't look after the island,' he remarked. 'I can look after myself but I can't look after everybody here.' He cupped his head in his hands for a few moments, looking down at the ground.

'I can lead the people,' he continued, 'but if they won't follow, there's bugger all I can do about it.'

Moa Assam wandered in and sat down heavily, eyes bloodshot and weary. He winced as he held his head.

'You'll have to give the grog away,' I told him. 'You'll have to stick to milk.'

'No,' he replied. 'There's too many germs in milk.'

The sun began to wane, and I remembered that Delphine had spoken about a turtle concoction — a sort of stew — she was preparing for the evening meal. Before long, she called to us to 'come and get it'. The meal was all that I had imagined it would be. After we finished eating, some of the family sat and watched videotapes; the rest of us took up the coolest spot on the verandah and sat talking until late into the night.

Chapter 10

It was about ten the following morning when the barge came in. This barge was used to supply everything needed to sustain life on the island, which, of course, included the inevitable cartons of beer. As I watched the passengers disembarking, my eyes rivetted on a woman I hadn't seen in years. Her name was Dot, and she would have been about eighty-three years old by then. For many years she had been a station cook out west, but had a falling out with her employer. She then specialised in relief cooking, going to whichever station needed a temporary replacement while the regular cook was ill or off on a holiday. She had kept in close touch with the stock and station agents in various country towns to whom graziers would apply for employees seeking employment. I waited until she had collected her bags of shopping — things were cheaper in Townsville — then approached her. At first she didn't recognise me but on hearing my name quickly recalled our past association. She lived just a little way up the road and I walked along with her, assisting her with her plastic bags. Her house was only small, but neat and tidy. Everything she needed for a reasonably comfortable life was in the place: lounge suite, dining table and chairs, refrigerator, and a television set and video recorder which took pride of place at the front of the lounge.

'Come and sit down, Bill,' she invited, as she began putting her groceries into a cabinet. 'I'll make a cup of tea in a minute.'

It was refreshing to be promised a cup of tea instead of the usual beer, but that was only to be expected from a real 'bushie'. She wasn't a small woman, but was quite well proportioned and appeared to be as strong as an ox, with huge forearms and squared shoulders. She wasn't all that black either; she would be regarded as 'coloured'. Her dress and demeanour would have made her acceptable in the most elite of white society.

The electric jug duly boiled and soon we were both ensconced in lounge chairs, talking about the old times. It occurred to me that Dot's vast experience on cattle stations must have given her a wealth of knowledge about life in western Queensland.

'You must have had some odd experiences during your time as a station cook,' I tested her. She pursed her lips for a moment.

'I'd certainly say so,' she replied, gingerly sipping her hot tea. She waited for me to continue.

'Does anything come immediately to mind?' I asked.

'I can remember one place where the station manager was a madman. Just a madman. There was no doubt about it.' She thought a bit before continuing. 'I just don't know whether it was the full moon or not but that is when these things used to happen. His wife was terrified of him.'

'Terrified of him?' I queried.

'Ooo, yes,' she affirmed. 'I'll never forget the night she came into the kitchen, covered in blood.' Dot could see the puzzled look on my face and gave a faint smile.

'Perhaps I'd better explain,' she said, brushing some crumbs onto her plate. 'Well,' she began, 'there was this station manager, see; the one I just talked about. Everybody reckoned that, during the full moon, he went a bit queer. Anyway, this night we were just finishing up in the kitchen when — '

'We?'

'Yes. I had two helpers in the kitchen, Mary and her daughter-in-law. We were just putting the tucker in tins for the men down at the camp.' She looked at me again, knowing quite well that she would have to explain that bit, too. 'See, there used to be lots of leftovers and I used to take them down to where the men were camped. You know, sweets and anything like that.'

'What did you actually do with these leftovers?'

'Gave them to the blacks, the workers. You know, you'd get into the habit of cooking a lot more than was required so there would be a good bit left over.'

'You'd make sure there was always plenty for the blacks?'

'Yes,' she replied. 'Well, you've got to feed your own colour, haven't you? You won't let them go hungry. I'd take it all down and they would bring the dishes back in the morning. Well, this day the manager was out — he was fifty miles [80 kilometres] away on another station. She [the manager's wife] came into the kitchen and she had her nightie on. She was covered in blood.' Dot grimaced as she recalled the event. 'I'll never forget the look on that woman's face. She was a beautiful little girl, only about twenty-four. I dived forward and grabbed her and got her up onto the table. She said, "I'm haemorrhaging." I said, "Yes, I can see that!" I said to Mary, "Will you stay with her?" She just rolled her eyes in fear; she was so bloody scared, you see. So I asked the other girl — she was the only part-blood on the station, the rest were all full-bloods — if she would stay and she said she would, see.' Dot sipped her tea again before resuming. 'We rushed over to the house and got some big treacle tins and put them under one end of the bed. Then we rushed over to the kitchen and carried her back to her bed.'

'You put treacle tins under her bed?' I asked incredulously. 'What the hell for? Some sort of superstition?' Dot looked at me with a puzzled look.

'No,' she said, as kindly as she could. 'You see, when anyone is haemorrhaging, you raise the foot of the bed.'

'I see,' I said, foolishly, 'to make the bottom of the bed higher.' I felt an absolute bloody idiot. Superstition, indeed! How many times had I raised a wounded limb in order to stem the flow of blood?

'When I got her comfortable, I rang Cleanskin [the outstation] and tried to get hold of him.'

'Who? The doctor?'

'No, her husband,' Dot replied. 'Anyway, I got him on the phone. See, he was the manager of the station and you can't do anything without the manager's permission. He said, "Well, if it was a calf, I'd cut it with a knife".' Dot threw back her head in an expression of disgust.

'He said that about his own wife?'

'Yes.'

'He'd be a miserable bastard, wouldn't he?' I remarked. 'If he did that to his wife, what would he do to a blackfellow?' The question didn't bear thinking about.

'All the camp were in and they all heard it,' Dot said. 'Then he hung up!'

She was visibly shaken at the memory because she was a very compassionate and forbearing woman, and the act she had just described revolted her. 'After that — well, I couldn't get any help from *him*, so I got in touch with Normanton where there was a nurse, but she was on the other side of the river, about eighty miles away and there was no possibility of getting her.' Dot's lips compressed, conveying the urgency of it all.

'She was a white nurse?'

'Oh, yes, she was a white nurse. She was on a station, there. See, a lot of station owners married nurses. I then contacted the Matron at Normanton and told her what was happening, and she asked me if I had been in touch with Mr P, the manager. I told her I had and what he had said. She said, "What?" and I told her again, "That is what he said: he'd cut it with a knife". Of course,' Dot confided, 'she's RH negative; the third child is the worst. The Matron said, "I want you to lift the bed up," and I told her that had already been done. I told her about the treacle tins. The Matron said, "Now I want you to pack her".'

Dot gave an embarrassed cough and then continued, 'I said to the Matron, "I don't know anything about that". The Matron said, "Well, you get the box [the Flying Doctor kit], everything is numbered". She told me to look for number one. So, I go to get the box but he's got it locked and he's got the bloody key! So we have to jemmy the thing open. Mary was so frightened that she was only one step behind me; every step I took, she was there.' Dot began laughing again at the memory, which now, of course, seemed funny but it had certainly been no joke at the time.

'Anyway,' Dot continued, 'I got this box open and I talked to the Matron about this packing business. I told her that I might do more harm that good. I wasn't very keen on this plugging a woman — not keen at all.' She held her head to one side, recapturing those rough and tough days in the outback.

'She told me to get all the treacle tins I could and put sump oil into them,' Dot continued. 'The only place I could get them was down on the rubbish dump. You know, the snakes are bloody bad there too. So are the spiders. Anyway, we found these tins and filled them up with oil and rags. These tins were to be makeshift lights to guide in the Flying Doctor's aircraft. I said to Mary, "You put them down one side of the landing strip and I'll put them down the other side".' Dot threw up her hands in delight as she recalled Mary's reactions to that suggestion.

'No, no,' Dot laughed, 'she wasn't going to do that. Mary wasn't going to leave my side for a second! Mary said, "No, missus. We put the tins down this side and then we put 'im down the other side". The Matron told me to train a light on the windsock so the pilot could see it. Well, you should have seen us. We'd race around, putting down a few lights, then race up to the house to see how the patient was; then race back down again and put out some more tins.' Her large frame heaved with laughter. She sipped her tea which, by now, had become cold, and pulled a face, as I knew she would. Cold, sweet tea tastes terrible.

'Listen, Bill,' she said, getting up from her chair, 'I'll put the jug on and make a fresh cup of tea.'

It wasn't long before she returned with two cups of steaming hot tea. 'Now where was I?' she mused, as she sat down again. 'Oh, yes,' she remembered, 'we were putting out these lights for the Flying Doctor. Well, this went on for hours. Luckily, Mrs P stopped haemorrhaging, but she was semiconscious. I kept ringing Normanton. Of course they weren't getting any sleep either, with all this ringing up all the time.' Dot sipped her tea as she gazed at the ceiling.

'The Matron said she was coming out with the Flying Doctor and they arrived just before first light. I shone the big torch on the windsock and they landed without any trouble at all. The doctor and the Matron examined her, and the doctor said, "Now, I'm going to take you back with me". She said, "Oh, no. I couldn't do that. Jack isn't here". The Matron said, "But you've *got* to come".'

'Was she frightened to go because her husband wasn't there?' I asked.

'Frightened?' Dot replied. 'He would have belted the bloody ears off her. He was a terrible man. So she wouldn't go without his permission.' Dot threw a look of disgust at me. I hoped she didn't think that all men were the same.

'I just can't think of the Matron's name,' she mused. 'She was very well known.' She gave a chuckle. 'Her husband was a mailman and he was just as tough as she was. He'd go out and he'd get that bloody mail through crocodile creeks and every other damn thing, no matter what.'

'What happened to the station manager's wife?' I enquired.

'When he came back from the outstation, he told her, "No! You can't go".'

'Even though she was critically ill?'

'Yes. But she was over the worst part. She wasn't haemorrhaging and the miscarriage had not taken place.'

'He must have been a miserable bastard,' I said.

'He was a terrible man,' Dot agreed. 'Anyway, the next thing his mother arrived on the scene. Well, she wasn't a nurse and we didn't like one another . . . And then he started a new caper; you never knew what was coming next.' Dot breathed deeply as she thought about her former employer. 'I put an order in for kitchen supplies and he ignored it; he wouldn't give us any food. There was Bronco [the rouseabout] and the horse breaker, besides us three in the kitchen. They were — '

'When you say he wouldn't give you any food, do you mean out of the store?'

'Out of the stores, yes. We were getting down so low in tucker and the day came when all I had was damper. I sent some over to his mother. She came over with all flags flying and she said, "What do you mean by only sending over damper?" I said, "Well, I haven't got anything else. Have a look for yourself". All the tins were empty; all the bins and cupboards were empty, and I said to her, "He hasn't given us anything for a fortnight". I said, "You've been eating over there but we're very short here. I think it's disgusting that the staff haven't been given any food". She went back, and the next thing I saw him come out like a bull out of a gate and into the store. He was throwing stuff left, right and centre! He put it all into boxes and brought it over. We've never had such an amount in the kitchen! Everyone ate again. That was the only good thing that happened.'

As Dot drank the last of her tea, she suddenly smiled again. 'We wanted some flour one day so I went out to him and told him that I needed flour — see, to make the bread. He said, "You're not getting any bloody flour. You can take the sack, instead". I said, "Thanks very much!" The trouble was, I had a crook arm and I wasn't able to drive my car.'

'He sacked you on the spot, did he?' I laughed.

'Yes, over asking for bloody flour.'

'He must have been a madman alright,' I said to her.

'Well, I wasn't going to leave my car there. God knows what might have happened to it. Bronco said, "I've had this bastard, too. I'll drive you over to Normanton". See, there were no roads in those days, only bush tracks. So Bronco drove me to Normanton.' Dot stretched her arms and stifled a yawn.

I looked at my watch. It was almost 9 pm. I was feeling tired and she must have been too. After all, Dot was no longer young and we had been sitting there yarning for about five hours. I stood up to leave.

'You must be tired, Dot,' I said to her. 'How about we give it away for today? I'll pop in tomorrow.'

She frowned at me in mock annoyance and then gave a hearty laugh.

'Oh, no, Bill,' she said. 'I'm a real bushie. I could sit up and talk about the old times all night. Where was I?' I sat down again and lit a smoke.

'Well, OK,' I told her. 'You were telling me about how you got the arse and Bronco drove you to Normanton.'

'Ah, yes, that's right. I was in Normanton for a while and they wanted a cook at another station and they knew I was there so they rang me and asked me and I said, "Well, I've got a crook arm". They said, "It doesn't matter. We've got good girls in the kitchen". And they did, too. They were terrific. I went there and we managed everything alright.' She laughed again. She had quite a chuckling type of laugh which I found quite infectious. 'One day, with this one-arm business, I could no longer make bread; I couldn't put enough pressure on to knead it, you know, I used to put it on a chair against the table and mix the dough and then pull it over. So, Mary said — her name was Mary, too — "I hold that, missus". I said to her, "Get a good hold of it, Mary". Of course, it's pretty heavy and Mary dropped it; the whole bloody lot. Well, they laughed, you know. They're such happy people. This Mary, she was so clean too. She'd clean the cupboards every day if you let her. I said to her, "Never mind. We'll take it down to the camp [where the station hands were camped]". It was alright because the floor was always clean. They were lovable people. I've only ever met one that wasn't'. Dot screwed up her face at the thought of the one black person she hadn't liked. 'She used to fight with her own people; she was a real bitch. Her name was Betty. She was the only one that fought with her people. She'd been educated a little bit and she worked for the police, in the house'.

'It might have been the police who embittered her towards her own people,' I suggested.

'It could have been,' Dot replied, 'because she never got on with her own colour. I always had trouble with her. Whenever I asked her to do anything, she wouldn't. The other girls would, but not Betty.' She placed her hands under her chin and appeared to be in deep thought.

I didn't interrupt her, but sat thinking about the life she must have lived out on the cattle stations. It would have been a constant battle against dust, heat, flies, flood, rain-soaked firewood, late musters, weevils, and pompous and sanctimonious station managers. But, whatever the obstacles, as station cook she'd have had to see that the hot food was on the table!

'You know, Bill,' she was saying, 'it always makes me very angry when they talk about natives. They are a very, very honest people and very faithful.' She seemed to be getting upset. 'If you were to give them a bag of sugar, and you told them they wouldn't get any more sugar for a fortnight, they'd say, "You-i"; but they would go down to their camp and eat the sugar until it was all gone.'

'They would just eat it with their hands?'

'Yes. They are sweet-toothed people. It's the same with tea: you'd give this out to them daily, their tea and sugar — you know, enough for the day, you're not being mean or officious, you're — '

'It's just to ensure that they get a regular supply,' I finished.

'Yes, that's right,' she said. 'It's well known that Aborigines will sit down and eat sugar till the cows come home.'

'No,' Dot repeated, 'it's not being mean; it's like giving a kid a bag full of lollies.' She looked at me squarely. 'I've never known them to take anything out of the kitchen. The groceries are always there, and so is everything else. Sometimes they might just look — it might be a tin of jam, or something. They don't say anything to you, they just keep looking, which gives you the impression that the tin of jam would be better in their camp. They were very honest and trustworthy.'

'Tom Petrie found that too,' I informed her. 'He had his place near Strathpine in the early days, in the 1800s. He could go away for a week and trust his Aboriginal workers. They wouldn't touch a thing, not even his tobacco. They even looked after his cattle and put them away at night for him. They had the full run of his place.'

'Oh, yes, of course. I've never had trouble with them.'

Dot rose from her chair and headed towards a small glass-fronted cabinet. She withdrew an old ragged photo album from it and returned to her seat.

'That Mary,' she reminisced, 'I hated parting with her because she was such a lovely person.' Dot's eyes narrowed. 'But I wouldn't have crossed Mary's tracks for the world!'

'Tough woman, was she?'

'She was dominant. She ruled that tribe there. She was the boss woman.' Dot browsed through the album then jabbed her finger onto one of the pictures.

'There.' She moved the album closer to me. 'That's Mary. That's my old kitchen mate. Black as the ace of spades, isn't she?' I peered closely at the picture and saw a fat, smiling face with very few teeth. The face exuded friendship and happiness. Dot poked her finger onto another photograph which was brown and stained with age.

'That's Bronco,' she informed me. 'He's the one that drove me into Normanton after I got the sack that time.' Dot studied the picture and smiled. Even though she appeared happy, I fancied I detected a wetness creeping into her eyes. Memories — memories of past pleasures, and sorrows — quite often cause eyes to sting a bit. But we are expected to face such nostalgic moments with stoicism, and say 'Ah, they were the good old days'. I often think that the only reason we say they were 'the good old days' is that they are gone.

Dot continued flipping over the pages and scrutinising the pictures.

'There are some here I don't even remember. Shameful,' she said idly. Some of the pictures must have been about sixty years old — why shouldn't she find them unfamiliar, mere apparitions of long ago?

She put the album away carefully. I had been right in thinking I saw moisture in her eyes: on returning to her chair she drew out a small hanky and dabbed her eyes. She gave a slight, embarrassed smile and blinked quickly several times.

'Ah, Bill,' she sighed, 'they were the days.'

'What were the working conditions like on that station, Dot?' I asked her.

She bit her bottom lip gently.

'The boss was a very tough man,' she replied, 'got on with him though. He was a Vestey's man.'

'One of the Bovril mob, eh?' I remarked. (Lord Vestey was managing director of the English company that made Bovril.)

'Mmm,' she mused, 'He *was* tough. He'd have no drink on the place. There were two big camps there with about forty in each camp.' She inclined her head to emphasise her words.

'Were they all blacks?'

'No, there were a few whites there. The overseer was white and he was useless. Even the boys [black station hands] used to say that the best bloke to be overseer was old Jock; but he couldn't be overseer because he was black. See, these white overseers used to go out and get lost and they would have to send the blacks out to find them.' She gave another look of disgust.

'I had good girls in the kitchen,' she went on. 'One was old Minnie. She couldn't speak English and she had claws; she didn't have hands, she had claws.' Dot bent her fingers into a claw shape. 'The first morning I was there the manager came down. I was in the kitchen, around four o'clock. See, on the stations, you've got to have that meal ready at piccaninny [first light] because they can only work the cattle until about nine o'clock because of the heat, and they can only start again about four in the afternoon. The cattle would be kept in coolers [shaded yards] during the time between. Sometimes they were called "settling paddocks". Some of these places would have about thirty thousand head of cattle. The ticks were bad there and they had to dip the cattle quite often.'

Dot paused in her narrative and smiled to herself.

'You know,' she continued, 'they paid two thousand guineas for the Grand Champion bull at the Sydney Show and brought him up there. They also bought a lousy little bull worth about eight hundred guineas; used to love carrots — he'd come up to the kitchen and bawl until you gave the silly bugger a carrot. He got a hernia.' She laughed at the memory. 'Well, they flew a vet out to the station from Townsville and saved the [little] bull's life. The two thousand guinea bull was given no attention at all, even though he was covered in ticks. There used to be a bloke out there whose job it was to look after these bulls.' Suddenly, Dot burst into a full-bellied laugh. 'They used to call him "Shampoo Charlie".' She giggled again. 'See, he had to currycomb and wash these bulls.' Dot pretended to be snobbish, emulating Shampoo Charlie. 'He thought he was real posh.'

'Sounds like the cattle got better treatment than the blacks,' I said to her.

She ignored my remark. 'The strange thing was that if they got ticks they didn't lift a finger to help them, except dip them; if they died, they died. The manager told me that if a bull died from ticks — that is, if ticks affected them — their progeny wouldn't be any good.'

'Because of ticks?'

'Yes. If they can't survive that tick fever, they'd be no good for breeding. They'd always be sickly.'

'Sort of survival of the fittest, eh?'

'Yes, that's right,' Dot agreed. 'Poor old Shampoo Charlie: he had to keep all the burrs and rubbish off the bulls. Well, after all, you just couldn't take them away from their beautiful stables that they were brought up in and dump them out in the sticks — it was a bit of a change.' Dot scratched her head lightly and frowned.

'Where was I before I got caught up with these bloody bulls?' she asked.

'You were telling me about Minnie.'

'Ah, yes, Minnie — she was the one who couldn't speak English.'

'Was Minnie in the kitchen?' I enquired.

'No. Minnie was in the garden really. She was pretty old. She was married to Paddy — he was a very old blackfellow, too. They came from Doomagee mission. My kitchen girl was Jessie — the manager used to sleep with Jessie because his wife was mad!'

At this point, Dot began to roar with laughter again, her sides heaved and she threw back her head in uncontrollable mirth. I waited a while for her to settle a bit.

'What's the joke?' I asked her then.

'Well, it's really funny,' she began to explain. 'She [his wife] used to put talcum powder in her bed to attract him. He couldn't stand this so he slept with Jessie. He'd come down every morning and tell me what his wife wanted for breakfast. I didn't know what his wife was like; I couldn't afford the time because I had to make eighteen loaves of bread every day and that takes some making!'

'Every day?'

'Well, yes. It doesn't keep up there and there were a lot of men there. Actually, that station was like a little town; there were streets in it. There were four natives and there were four over in the house — there was eight — and myself and the cowboy: that made ten; but the others needed bread, too. The overseer would get a loaf of bread; there was the blacksmith and the saddler and his family — they'd get a couple of loaves. There wouldn't be any left. Anyway, it would go mouldy — or, ropey, as they called it. I was told not to give the outside black workers anything because there was a lot of tucker around the place that they could get for themselves.'

'Who told you this? The manager?'

'Yes, the manager. He was rather a decent bloke in a way but he hated blacks.' She held her head to one side, thinking. She scratched her cheek and looked slightly towards the ceiling.

'Well, he didn't actually *hate* them — he used to sleep with Jessie. This colour bar, when you go into it, gives me the shits! It didn't matter what I gave them; if I gave them a bit of damper and corned beef, that was enough. Well, it wasn't in *my* book! Anyhow, you don't argue with them when they give you these instructions; as long as they're getting what they want over at the house, they don't bother to come and check. Anyway, I had been feeding them up on good tucker, and one day Minnie came in and grabbed me by the arm, sinking her bloody talons into me. I thought, "What have I done?" She went, "Yabba-yabba-yabba" and I couldn't make out what was wrong. "She's thanking you," Jessie told me. "The other cook never fed us." Just imagine: never fed them! I used to say to them, "Here, cut the meat up and take it". Well, the cheapest thing on a cattle station is meat. There were over thirty thousand head there. The cold rooms were always full of it. I'd give them all kinds of sweets, too. It was usually sago or tapioca, stuff like that. Then you'd have your big days when you made your plum pudding up in treacle tins. I'd give them tins of pudding and custard. They loved it. It wasn't costing the station much because they were getting cheap labour. I think the girls were getting four pounds a month, and even then they weren't getting it given to them: it had to go to the police for them to look after. And those girls worked bloody hard. For instance, over in the house there were ninety windows that had to be cleaned a couple of times a week. Ninety bloody windows — and most of them were upstairs. I've never been upstairs so I don't know what else was up there to be cleaned. One day I discovered that there was a piano there. The place was so large that I'd never noticed it before.' Dot waited for my reaction. I didn't disappoint her: I let my bottom jaw drop a little.

'Then there was this hand-operated [sewing] machine. Well, talk about funny! See, the woman who did the sewing used to get old Minnie to turn the handle and she expected Minnie to stop when she wanted it stopped. The trouble was, Minnie had no idea when she was supposed to stop and you'd hear yells coming from the sewing room. It was as funny as a circus to watch.'

By now, we had finished off our cups of tea and, like a true bushie, Dot went into the kitchen and made more, this time in a huge pot. She was settling in for an all-night sitting.

'Have another cuppa, Bill,' she said, as she filled my cup. 'They reckon it's good for the kidneys, which reminds me.'

She left the room for a few moments. I was wondering where she had got to when I heard the toilet flush. When she returned I went out too.

It wasn't long before another event from the past sprang into her mind and, once again, she doubled up with mirth.

'There was a plague of locusts there once,' she began. 'Well, you've never seen anything so funny in your life. See, all the blacks were called out and given sticks to kill the grasshoppers. You couldn't see the place for grasshoppers; it was just like a snowstorm.' She clicked her tongue as she finished the sentence. 'You can't kill a plague of grasshoppers with bloody sticks.' She laughed incredulously. 'Even the blackfellows thought they were going mad. They even had the bookkeeper out in the paddock killing grasshoppers.' Dot scowled at the mention of the bookkeeper, and her eyes blazed momentarily.

'This bookkeeper,' she said bitterly, 'he was a real, mean miserable hound. He went to try his luck with Jessie. She was a powerful woman and she just picked him up and threw him — threw him out of her room. He had skin off everywhere. He came along next morning feeling sick and sorry for himself and got nothing for his trouble. Ah, but he was a mean ... ' Obviously she couldn't find adequate words to express her feelings.

'He was a very dishonest man, he was. There was this fellow Ernie there whose parents had died. I think his mother had died at childbirth; his father was a timber cutter. He took this child out and reared him in the timber camp, but got killed when the boy was about seven years old. By this time Ernie was able to make tea — you know, he was the wood and water joey around the camp; he was brought up that way. He'd never had a day's education in his life. When he grew up, he went out there. The place was overrun with brumbies and he used to go out brumbie shooting and Mactaggarts used to buy the hair.' (Mactaggarts was a Queensland stock and station agent.)

'The hair?'

'Yes, the hair. The tail and the mane — you know.'

'Oh, yes, I see.'

'Well, he'd send this hair down, see. This bookkeeper used to do the correspondence for him because he couldn't read or write. Well, the bookkeeper got stung one day while he was out fishing and he collapsed on the way back. They had to carry him back. They got the doctor out and he was taken to hospital and this correspondence came through for Ernie, but he couldn't read it. He brought it over to me to read. I read it to him and this bookkeeper had been taking him down. The money that Mactaggarts were paying for his hair — well, Ernie was only getting a fraction of what Mactaggarts were paying him for this hair.'

'Well, I'll be buggered!' I was staggered. You just don't *do* that out in the bush. Dot saw the look of disbelief on my face and nodded to emphasise her words. If anybody had seen us they'd have thought we were a couple of ratbags: Dot nodding her head slowly up and down, and me slowly shaking mine.

'I used to do his correspondence after that. You see, whenever a cheque from Mactaggarts arrived, the bookkeeper would give him one of his and keep the cheque from Mactaggarts. It was a cheap and lousy trick.'

Dot rose and crossed to the cabinet again. She returned with the photograph album and thumbed through its pages until she found what she was looking for. She brought it over to me and jabbed a finger onto one faded photograph.

'I just thought I'd show you this,' she remarked. 'This is a picture of a couple of girls when they were sick once.'

I looked at the photograph, which showed three Aboriginal girls lying on what appeared to be bags.

'What's wrong with them?' I asked. 'They look miserable.'

'That's when the flu hit the station. See, what happened was, a crowd of black people came over from Robinson River in the Northern Territory to pick up some bulls ... for the station where they worked. There were a couple of white people with them. The blacks here on the station didn't trust the blacks from Robinson River — they were a Territory crowd and there was a great to-do in the blacks' camp. They weren't friendly at all, but what they *did* bring with them, and left, was the flu. It was that Asian flu. Some of us healthy ones were asked to go around and give the sick ones some tablets. I needed more tablets, so I went over to the homestead to get some. The girls were lying on the kitchen floor on bags. They *were* sick. They had diarrhoea, too. The flies were dreadful. The manager's wife said, "I'm not going to give them any pills". I said, "But you've got them there". She said, "Yes, but what if Joe gets sick? We won't have any for Joe". Joe was her husband. I said, "Well, get the Flying Doctor out and take them away or they'll die". She said, "Oh, no, they won't die. But they're not getting any pills." Now ... ;' Dot took on a more serious attitude, 'in those days if you were to interfere with the ruling of the manager over the blacks, you could be arrested. Did you know that, Bill?'

'Yes,' I replied, 'it was covered by the Queensland *Aborigines Act*.' (This Act was repealed in 1984.)

'I could not interfere,' Dot said. 'I had no access to the pedal radio to let the doctor know about the condition of these people and I doubt if they would have listened to me anyway. I gave out all the pills that I had and Maisy, one of my kitchen helpers, came over to me and said, "Christ, missus; they won't die. They're too lazy to die!" In the end they shifted them out of the kitchen and put them about twenty yards away and they were still lying out there, day and night. It was summer so they were never cold. That's where they stayed, the poor bastards, and they all survived.'

'Every one of them?'

'Yes, they all survived. I used to make soup and take it down and give it to them, the poor devils.'

Dot frowned and shook her head, her eyes staring at the floor.

'See, Bill,' she continued, 'they weren't what you would call cruel to the blacks, just bloody inconsiderate. The — well, some — station-owners reckon that the blacks weren't *worth* treating. It was the accepted thing in those days. It's difficult to understand. A couple of the blacks were given a snort of rum by some of the friendlier whites but the station manager got onto it. He wouldn't allow drink on the place, remember? He came down — I could hear him coming — and he wanted to know how grog got into the camp, you see. Well, nobody knew. You know what, Bill? He sacked the whole bloody camp!' She half-inclined her head as she looked at me.

'You know,' she stressed, 'a manager has to think twice, or half a dozen times, before sacking a camp. It's a dangerous thing to do and he's got to be very careful. It's marvellous how a match can drop. It could burn the whole bloody place down. Thousands of acres could be burnt out. But, anyway, he came down and sacked the lot. They were bringing taxis out from Mt Isa and Cloncurry to take them away. But there still was no guarantee that someone wouldn't flick a match or a cigarette butt into the dry grass. Everyone was holding their breath.'

'Who paid for the taxis?' I asked her.

'Oh, the men. They had to be off the place; they got instant notice. The bookkeeper was called out of bed to write the cheques. They were all gone by eleven o'clock that night. I was instructed that there was no food to go out of the kitchen for them. Of course, it wasn't part of my job to have anything to do with them; they had their camp cook down there and he hadn't been sacked so it was in their court as to whether he fed them or not. I don't think they'd want a feed after a shock like that.' She laughed, but the laugh was soon replaced by a grim set of her jaws.

'It's easy to laugh now,' she observed, 'but they were bloody tough times, believe me.'

'Dot,' I asked, 'this camp that was sacked; were they blacks?'

'No, they were whites,' Dot replied. 'There were no blacks in those camps. There may have been a few half-castes but they wouldn't be on the same wages as the white workers. The girls I had helping me were black. And there was Bronco, of course; he was a half-caste. We all ate together in the kitchen.' Dot lowered her voice. 'Actually, this was against the rules because in those days blacks were not allowed to eat with whites and whites were not allowed to eat with blacks, and white workers were not allowed to eat with the management.'

'Sort of, class distinction?' I observed.

'Oh, yes,' Dot agreed. 'But the funny thing was, black girls could serve meals up to whites but weren't allowed to do anything else.' She bent her head again, smiling sardonically. 'Whites used to take young black girls to bed with them; that was considered alright.' She clicked her tongue at the thought of the double standards.

'Talking about black girls serving whites at the table,' she sniggered, 'I'll never forget the time the Governor was coming out to the station. Governor Henry Abel-Smith it was. The station manager's wife really let her hair down on that occasion. She could sew a bit and she wanted to put on a swank act for the Governor. She came over to the kitchen to talk to me. She told me that Jessie was promoted to waitress and that she was going to make a uniform for her. It was to be a green uniform and a white apron with applique down the sides, and headgear with the station name across the top, and little turn-back sleeves with the name on them. There was a great to-do about this. So she measured Jessie up so she would be all dressed up when the big day arrived. Now, Bill,' she giggled, 'this Jessie was a big woman and she had enormous feet. She always wore a big military hat, I think she slept in the thing. Anyway, the day finally came, the Governor arrived. He was only coming for lunch. All the best silver had to be brought out, and to lift some of these dishes, you've got to use two hands because it is so heavy. It was old too, because it was what they used back in the colonial days. It was beautiful stuff. God knows what it was worth. Then she decided that Jessie would have to wear a bra. She finds one her size and gives it to her.' Dot began to chuckle again.

'Of course,' Dot added disparagingly, 'it was only proper that Jessie would wear footwear — white boots of all things. So everything was ready to go over; all the food was nicely placed in the dishes. It was midday and they were going to have a hot meal, three courses: soup, meat and vegetables, and sweets. In comes Jessie to collect it. Well, you've never seen anything so funny in your life! The bra was on the *outside* — Jessie said she wasn't going to have that thing underneath; it was too pretty — and that bloody old hat was shoved down onto her head, crushing that beautiful little peak cap — and the lovely white boots had gone! Instead, there were her big black feet. Well, it's not for me to interfere. So in she goes! Well, there were the manager and wife, the bookkeeper, the Governor and his aide-de-camp, and the pilot; the Shire Clerk and his wife were also there. When she walked in, no one turned an eyelid.'

'It must have almost caused a riot,' I remarked. 'They surely must have laughed about the whole thing.'

'Well, you can't dress black people up in stupid things like that,' she agreed. 'It was a very nice thought, I suppose, but you can't turn people around like that. Old Sir Henry, he was the easiest joker in the world. He'd come over to the kitchen and thank you and shake hands with you. I met him on a couple of occasions. He loved roast beef and he loved corned beef, and plenty of it. He didn't want these fancy dishes. He was sick of chicken. He could get that sort of stuff anywhere. He wanted a good feed of roast beef that came from the Gulf.'

Dot stretched her arms and tightened her shoulders. It occurred to me once again that she must be tired. But when I told her that I would go and return again another time, she would have none of it. She lived alone and I think she wanted to talk for as long as possible because, being often in Townsville, she apparently didn't receive many visitors. Well, I was always a good listener. I had to admire her. She was one of the old breed, a dinky-di bush woman who had put up with all types of hardships but had carried on regardless. Rough and thankless as the lifestyle had been, however, the roughness hadn't rubbed off on her. She always carried herself with elegance and aplomb.

She continued, 'The first cattle station I went onto had Aboriginal workers.'

'All Aborigines?'

'No, the manager and the overseer and the head stockman were white,' she replied. 'But the Aborigines were treated badly.'

'Was it a big camp?'

'About fifteen,' she answered. 'That was the station I was telling you about before, where the manager was a madman, at full moon he'd do the most ridiculous things. For instance, he'd go out with a gun and blaze away at the moon.'

'Strike a light!' I joked. 'Did he ever hit it?'

She laughed lightly at my attempted humour. 'One night I went out to the kitchen to stoke the fire up, my room was beside the kitchen. I noticed movement in the corner, and there he was, just standing there. I was in my nightie and I demanded to know what he was doing there. He didn't answer; he just went away. When I broke my arm — I broke it by falling down the stairs — he tied my arm up. He got two pieces of packing case and put them on my arm, one front and one back. He bound it up tight and the splinters from the boards were sticking into my arm and the swelling was making it worse. At first light, the doctor came and he undid the bandage and my arm was bleeding where the splinters were being forced into it. Talk about a mad bastard!'

I thought it was time to change the subject. 'What about the Flying Doctor? Was he the pilot also?'

'No, the pilot was a Bush Pilot. They were stationed in Cairns but there was always someone at Normanton. The Matron there was a very efficient woman.' She stopped speaking, and waved her arm in a gesture of urgency. 'But I want to tell you about this bloke I saw in the kitchen. When you get into your nightie, you take everything off then slip into your nightie. I'd got into bed and settled down when I heard these footsteps. There was only one man in the camp and that was the mechanic.'

She leaned over closer to me and hushed her voice. 'Well, I jumped out of bed and looked out the window and I saw the mechanic just coming out of the men's quarters. Well, he couldn't have got from my place over to his place in that short space of time — only a few seconds — and the only other man around was old Paddy and he never wore boots; so that left the manager!' She looked at me as I imagine Sherlock Holmes would have looked at Dr Watson: knowing, mysterious, smart-arse. 'So, at piccaninny, I went down there and there were all these cigarette butts and high-heeled boot marks. I thought, "You bastard!" Now, that man had stood there and watched me, at fifty years of age, get undressed! And he was a young man of twenty-eight.'

'Struth,' I obliged her. 'Bloody hell, eh?'

'There was something wrong with him . . . and the moon was coming full.'

'You might have been a good sort,' I suggested impishly. 'You never know. You might have had oomph!'

She looked at me sedately and smiled ever so slightly. 'Well,' she said modestly, 'I still had my figure — even at fifty.' She looked down at her ample waist. 'I wasn't like I am now.' She laughed to hide her embarrassment. 'He had a beautiful young wife too. And she had lovely brown eyes — with a lot of black around them too, where he used to belt her up.'

I changed the subject once more. 'How do you like it here, on Palm Island?' I asked her.

'Oh, I like it alright,' she replied. 'I couldn't live on the mainland — too many miserable white people.' Her eyes were looking around the table and came to rest on the bowl of sugar. She reached out her hand and touched it. 'By gee, you know,' she remarked, 'looking at that sugar bowl brings back memories too.' I looked at the bowl.

'Doesn't sound very interesting, Dot,' I remarked.

'Well, it was on that station I told you about before. See, there was this sugar bowl on the kitchen table. It didn't look too clean and I told Mary to try and clean it up a bit. Mary stared at me with wide eyes. She would hardly look at it, let alone clean it. I knew then that there was something about it, something odd. I said to Mary again, "Clean that sugar bowl". She just rolled her eyes. There was no way Mary was going to touch that sugar bowl. It was a greyish colour and I had a net with shells around it to cover it with. I took it and gave it a good scrub but it was still no cleaner. One of the fellows came in one day and said, "How do you like Sambo?" I said, "Sambo? Who's Sambo?" He pointed to the sugar bowl and said, "That". It turned out to be a blackfellow's skull! It had a piece of wood on the bottom of it to make it stand straight.'

'What did you say when you found out it was a skull?' I asked.

She frumped up her shoulders and puffed her cheeks. 'I said, "Get that dirty, filthy thing out of here!" I was furious. It was taken away and buried. There was that scandal, too, about that dentist who took those skeletons of babies from the Carnarvon Ranges. It was in the papers at the time.'

'What skeletons were they, Dot?'

'Well, they were wrapped in bark. He had one skeleton in his surgery and the other one in his home.'

'What became of the skeletons? Do you know?'

'I don't know,' Dot admitted. 'I really don't know what became of them.'

I was anxious to get off the subject of skulls and skeletons. Not my kettle of fish at all! 'You were telling me about the blacks on the first station you worked on. Were they treated alright?'

'No way,' she replied, hastily. 'They were cruel to them. Talk about mistreatment! The little boys, for instance, these little nine-year-olds and eleven-year-olds were like frogs sitting on the horses. They were made to work. Just imagine what those big horses were doing to their joints, their little legs. The poor little buggers used to get tired. The overseer was a real bastard; he used to get the stockwhip and get stuck into them with it. He use to say "That livens the little black bastards up". He used to get a lot of fun out of it, too. That was cruelty; just like those cruel mongrels that auctioned off that girl.'

'Hey?' My attention snapped back to her words. 'What's that? Auctioning a girl?'

'Yes, it happened,' Dot replied. 'I was in the kitchen. Mary was getting very agitated. I hadn't done anything to her or said anything to her. She was busy cleaning up the cigarette butts because she used to keep them for herself.'

'To smoke?'

'Yes, to smoke.' Dot looked at me over the top of her spectacles as if to say, why do you ask such a stupid bloody question? 'You couldn't throw butts away. But she wasn't interested in the butts this night. The fellows had their heads together and eventually one of them came out and said, "The dirty bastards!" and he slammed the door as he went out. I thought, "What the bloody hell is wrong with him?" Then Mary shot out of the kitchen like a bullet, and after a while I heard a lot of laughter going on in the station livingroom. The manager came over and I heard him say, "I'll take a couple of tickets". Then they all went away, back to their quarters.'

Dot paused for a moment. I could tell she was leading up to a dramatic end to her story. 'Around about 10 o'clock,' she continued, 'there was this bloody big din; it was a terrible noise. Yells and screams and so on.' She stopped again and looked at me . . . I think just to tantalise me and force me to ask her more about it.

'Well, go on,' I didn't disappoint her, 'what had happened?'

'Well,' she said, satisfied that her yarn was having the desired effect, 'they'd raffled off this young black girl at a quid a ticket and the bloke that won it had gone down to collect his prize. That's why Mary had been agitated: she knew what was going on. But Mary had organised everything and all the blacks in the camp were waiting inside for him. When he arrived, they pulled him inside and then they really got stuck into him. Well, Bill,' she sighed, 'I don't know if you've seen black women fight with sticks, but it's sickening. They played "Larry Dooley" up and down his body. They broke his collarbone; they broke his arm and they broke his ribs; and then Mary — she was a powerful woman — and the rest of them just threw him out, broken bones and all. You should have heard the screams of that fellow.'

'Was he just one of the station hands?' I enquired.

'Yes,' Dot nodded. 'He was a ringer — but his prize wasn't what he expected. They called the Flying Doctor and they took him into Cloncurry. He must have learnt a lesson because he didn't come back all the time I was there. They really done him over.'

Dot poured out more tea from the huge pot that was keeping warm on the small gas stove. It was well brewed by now but it was still welcome. 'There was a mob of wandering blacks there too, at the time. They saw it all. They didn't speak to anyone. Mary had come back [to the kitchen] and asked them if they were hungry. They were not hungry because there was a stack of food around for them. The rivers around there were full of barramundi and they used to pounce on the small crocodiles with stones. What they wanted was tea and sugar, and I told them I would give them some after dark, when no one with big eyes and loose tongues was around. Mary yelled out something to them in their own lingo and they moved off until later.'

Dot finished her tea and took her cup over to the sink and began to rinse it. But before she had finished her task, she came back over to where I was, wiping her hands on a small handcloth.

'Tell you another thing about those wandering blacks,' she said, 'they go absolutely mad over condensed milk. They can't get enough of it. Sometimes they mix it with water and drink it until they can't walk.'

'Well,' I observed, 'it's better than being full on beer or plonk. Or worse still, metho.'

'Oh, yes, certainly,' she agreed, with a nod. 'Anyhow, I gave them a big stack of condensed milk. There's always a ton of it on a station.'

'Did you take the milk down to them?'

'Yes. Well, there was a shed down there and I put the stuff in there. They wouldn't sleep in the hut because there was only one door on it and if a debil-debil came, there would be no way for them to get out.'

Dot's mind seemed far away for a moment, bringing back memories of the past. She straightened up and gave a little smile. Suddenly she was off on another tangent.

'You know, talking about that shed,' she recalled, 'that was where Mary went to get sick.'

'What do you mean, Dot?' I asked. 'Why would she want to get sick?'

'Well,' Dot began, 'Mary had a daughter in Normanton — about fourteen she was — and Mary wanted her daughter out on the station with her but the manager wouldn't allow it. But Mary was adamant she was going to get her out to there. So Mary, cunning bugger, put on a couple of cardigans and a man's military overcoat, a man's military hat, and big boots and she marched around the place all day and then went and sat in the boiling hot shed, just to make herself sick. Well, she became ill alright. When the plane came in on Thursday, she fooled them and said she wanted to go to the hospital in Normanton. Of course, as soon as she got on the plane she took off all these clothes and was better again in no time. But she got to Normanton. She was worried about her daughter because she lived in a camp with four hundred other blacks, and the whites used to hire taxis and take grog up to them. Of course, you know what for! Old Mary was petrified about her daughter.'

'Did the blacks resent the whites going up there in taxis?'

'I don't know,' Dot replied. 'I've never been to the camp. I don't think any money changed hands, only grog and tobacco. Anyway,' Dot continued, 'Mary was back on the next plane with her daughter. She kept her hidden away and the manager never found out about it.'

I asked Dot if she minded if I smoked in the house. She told me that she'd been among smokers all her life and it didn't bother her one bit. So I lit one up and settled back again, waiting for her to continue. She seemed to have no end of stories and experiences.

'This Mary,' Dot was off again, 'she had a big scar on her leg. I said to her one day, "Mary, how did you get that scar on your leg?" Mary looked at me and her eyes began to roll. It appeared she had been 'sung', but the witch-doctor [Kadaitcha man] happened to come along and got it out for her. There were these marks as big and as deep as your finger, so I quite believed her that this had happened.'

'What did the witch-doctor get out of her leg?'

'Well, Mary said it was a piece of iron.'

'It's unusual for it to be iron,' I told her. 'It's usually a stone or a piece of bone.'

'She told me it was iron, as far as I can remember,' Dot repeated. 'I wouldn't like to get on the wrong side of her,' Dot laughed. 'She ran that tribe with a rod of iron.'

Little wonder, I thought, that Mary was the boss. Working in the station kitchen, she was in a position to supply the tribe with quite a lot of food: sugar, meat, and unlimited supplies of leftover pudding (and Dot saw to it that there was always a considerable amount of excess pudding and tea). In fact, anything the tribe might fancy.

'Mary had a daughter-in-law,' Dot was saying. 'She was a useless girl. All she wanted to do was play with her baby. She would sit there and play with this little girl. I would give her little jobs like breaking up lumpy sugar with a hammer, but she would just sit and play with her baby. Her husband worked in the stock camp and I don't know whether he was ever flogged with a stockwhip but his little brothers were. This overseer used to flog them just to "smarten the little black bastards up a bit". One day the manager's little three-year-old daughter was playing on the lawn outside the staff diningroom when he rode up. Now he idolised this little girl. The little girl ran to meet him and he flicked that stockwhip at her to within an inch of her.'

Dot grimaced. 'He had this peculiar smile on his face. We all watched him; he never touched the child but the child was absolutely petrified with fear. Then the mother came out and took the little girl away. You know, that kid had nightmares for weeks after that. He was just a madman. There was no doubt about it. His wife was terrified of him too; and she was going to have her third child too.'

While we'd been sitting there for all these hours — it was now about 4 am — we hadn't noticed a storm approaching. Now a sudden streak of lightning and an enormous clap of thunder frightened the daylights out of us. Then the rain started, and the wind! The rain dropped in sheets and the coconut palms were so bent before the wind that I thought they must surely snap in two. Paper, cardboard cartons, and plastic bottles were being whirled around, stopping only when they became caught up in some fence. Then the wind would change completely and the articles would come flying back to their starting point. The storm didn't last long and soon the rays of the rising sun made kaleidoscopic patterns among the trees on the tops of the mountains. The rain cleared completely, and the day was fine and bright, all traces of pollution washed from the air. If you looked very carefully, you could even see the goats grazing on the steep slopes of Goat Island, a little to the east. I said goodbye to Dot and walked home along the muddy road, its gutters still running with the water coming down the sides of the mountains.

Chapter 11

I managed to get a few hours' sleep, but was up again, drinking tea, at about 9 am. I walked down to the administration building and knocked on Rick's door. A female staff member poked her head around the door and informed me that Rick had gone to some meeting on the mainland which, she said, he had arranged weeks ago and that he wouldn't be back for several days. I thanked her and returned to the grassy area beside the community hall, wondering if my face betrayed the anger I felt. Here I was, all the way from Brisbane to discuss producing a newsletter — at Rick's request — and at the appointed time he disappears for 'several days'. I sat and simmered for a while, lighting a smoke and crushing it out several times. Eventually, though, I lay back on the cool grass to consider my next move. I must have succumbed to the warm rays of the sun because I awoke to someone gently kicking on my ribs. I squinted up and saw that it was my old friend Bill Congoo, a soggy home-rolled cigarette hanging from his lips.

'Get up, you tired old bastard,' he greeted me jokingly. 'What, you think you in a 'oliday camp or something?' I started to sit up, but before I had reached an erect position, Bill had asked me for 'a decent fucking smoke!' I gave him one of my Hallmark cigarettes and he tossed his spit-soaked rollie onto the grass, watched closely by a couple of young kids. As one, they swooped on the filthy butt and scampered off.

'Hey, you young bastards,' Bill swore at them, 'I'll kick your arse for ya! You too young to smoke.' But the kids were far away by then.

'When did *you* start to smoke, Bill?' I asked him.

'Aw, about ten, I suppose.' He grinned as he took my point. 'But I was workin' then,' he defended. 'We all smoked.'

He sat down on the grass beside me and took off his shirt, or what remained of it, and brushed back his rough, greying hair with his hand. He was looking down towards the jetty where the first of the tourists were disembarking from a small tourist vessel. As I watched, his expression suddenly changed. He had grown old since my visit to the island in 1974. Deep creases ran down his thin face and, although he had shaved, patches of beard were visible where the razor had missed.

He looked very tired, very subdued. His life, like that of many others of his generation, had been harsh: a battle for survival against poverty, injustice, exploitation and all the other ingredients which cook up into the poison pie of racism.

'Want another smoke, Bill?'

I grinned as he took a cigarette from the packet I held out to him.

'How you know I want a smoke? You know me, eh?' he joked.

'Well, Bill,' I replied, 'I've known you for a bloody long time, old mate.'

My mind streaked back to the cruel way his wife had died. Odd, I thought, no one ever heard or read about it on the Australian mainland! Why was it, I wondered, that when someone set fire to him or herself in an overseas country such as India or Asia, it made world headlines, complete with gruesome television pictures, yet some poor black woman does the same thing on an Aboriginal reserve in Queensland, and not a word is said, or written. I shook my head slowly at the hopelessness of it all. Even earlier, in 1957, I'd since been told, Bill Congoo had been involved in a strike on Palm Island. A futile strike, as it turned out. It created some excitement and a brief taste of self-determination, but that was all. Industrial protection? Unions? There was none of it on Palm Island. Members of the Queensland Police Force were flown over to control the strike. They invaded the strikers' homes in the dead of night, dragged them out of bed and spirited them away to various Aboriginal reserves on the mainland. Bill Congoo was among them.

'You must have been here for a long time, Bill,' I commented. 'How long *have* you been here?'

'Aw, Christ! I don't know.' He shrugged his shoulders and tugged idly at the grass. 'Buggered if I know. I remember being here as a kid but I don't know where I come from.'

'Did you go to school when you came here?' I asked him.

'Nah,' he spat. 'No school. I worked for my tea.'

'Tea? What do you mean "tea"?'

'Tea! Fucking tea. You know what fucking tea is, don't you?'

'You cranky old bastard!' I scolded him. 'No more bloody smokes for you.' He smiled sheepishly at me.

'I'm a cranky old bastard, eh?' he conned.

'No, not really,' I smiled. 'What sort of work did you have to do for your rotten tea?' I could speak to Bill in this manner and he to me. We were really very good friends.

'I used to pick oysters off the rocks,' he informed me. 'Bags of the bloody things. Jeez, my fingers used to bleed.'

'Did you work for that Butler bloke?'

'Yes,' he replied. 'That's the bloke. How did you know?'

'A lot of young kids worked for him in the early days,' I told him. 'But they used to get a shilling a bag. Why didn't you?' He thought for a moment before replying.

'Too young,' he said. 'Young and stupid.' He made that typical motion of rubbing the palms of his hands together which, in blackfella lingo, means 'Have you got a smoke?'

Had I got a smoke! He knew bloody well I had a smoke. I placed the open packet on the ground between us.

'Have you got a charge [an alcoholic drink]?' I asked him.

'Where would I get a bloody charge from?' he replied. 'No money. Have you got any?'

'What's the good of you?' I chided. 'You're a dead loss.'

We both laughed at each other's words. He rose from the ground and looked longingly towards the pub. I rose also and followed his gaze.

'Come on,' I offered. 'Let's go and have a few beers.' We set off towards the hotel and it was only natural that, with his long, spindly legs, he would be well ahead of me. We sat in the pub for a few hours, swapping stories. The light began to fade at about the same time as my intemperance so, deliberately exaggerating my state of insobriety, I strode out the door and headed for my billet at Assam Clay's house.

A meeting was planned in Brisbane in a few days' time. It was a sort of land rights meeting; this time, the blacks were going to try and claim Musgrave Park, a nice, green oasis on the south side of Brisbane city. I decided to go down to the city and take part.

Chapter 12

I arrived back in Brisbane the day before the meeting was to be held, and wandered across the river to Musgrave Park to familiarise myself with the area. As I wandered aimlessly around I noticed an Aborigine walking towards me; I felt I had met him before somewhere. As he drew level with me, he stopped and looked at me, his dark, bushy eyebrows raised.

'Bill Rosser!' he blurted out. As soon as he spoke I recognised the voice of Don Murchinson, an old friend I hadn't seen in years. We shook hands, and Don outlined to me the Aborigines' new plan for claiming Musgrave Park. There had been quite some agitation to claim the park not long before. Actually, it was the favourite drinking spot, and home, of the 'goomies' — alcoholic derelicts, who drank cheap wine and methylated spirits — and very few whites were game enough to come near the park. This was not out of fear of violence from the blacks but rather because the goomies, in their tribal kindness, would buttonhole the interloper into either having a drink with them or buying a drink for them. As the drink consisted of a mixture of methylated spirits and orange cordial, there were seldom any takers. The blacks, wild, woolly, unkempt and usually half drunk, quite often practised throwing boomerangs in the park. On these occasions quite a large audience of white people would gather to watch the prowess of the throwers. But they were a cunning lot, these spectators. If a boomerang landed close to where a group of onlookers were standing, they would quickly turn away, pretending to be looking for street numbers. They were happy to watch the display, but they weren't at all anxious to be too close to a blackfellow which would be the case as the thrower came to collect his boomerang. But it was the blacks who had the big laugh: they would engineer their toss, not to return, but to land almost at the feet of some comely white girl who would redden as everybody stared at her to see if she was game enough to hold her ground. Some did, most didn't. Those who hastened away were met with howls of mirth from the blacks in the middle of the arena. Those blackfellows might have been goomies but they certainly weren't idiots!

On the appointed day of the meeting to 'claim Musgrave Park', a large mob of blacks turned up. I have no idea where they all came from because I am quite sure there weren't that many blacks in or near Brisbane. I had been away when the meeting was planned, and therefore had no inside information.

The meeting was a lively one with all the usual claims being made: there were blacks buried there so it must be a tribal burial ground; it was once a tribal fighting ground which contained 'much blood', so it was obviously a sacred site. One old bloke staggered over to the microphone and claimed that the land had been given to his ancestors by Captain Cook himself! It must be said that those boys certainly didn't lack initiative. Now, it is not for me to say, or to remark upon, what the original purpose of Musgrave Park was, but I must say I regarded the claim that the land was handed over by Captain Cook himself as pretty doubtful. I don't think he *got* that far, did he?

I arrived back at my motel at about 8.30 pm. There being nothing further to hold me in Brisbane, I booked a seat on the next morning's flight to Townsville. From there, I boarded the flimsy aircraft to Palm Island.

Chapter 13

Rick Clay was now back from his meeting on the mainland. I had intended to say a few well-chosen words to him for leaving me like a shag on a rock but, I thought, what would be gained? What was needed, if the plight of Palm Island, or its Chairman, was to be solved, was for the two of us to stick together. Rick was hoping for a good turn-up at the meeting he had organised, considering it to be a great leap forward in community relations, in particular, between the council and the community.

The meeting opened at 1 pm on the nominated day. Many of the residents had turned up with the proverbial blood in their eyes. In fact, a group calling itself the 'Palm Island Action Group' almost dripped blood! It seemed to me that their main and biggest problem was themselves. They moaned and griped about conditions on the island that didn't suit them, but they appeared to be doing little about the 'problems' other than to put the onus onto other people to solve or rectify them. One member of the action group chastised the council because a council member's daughter was given employment while the action group's daughter was not. She never considered the fact that the council member's daughter was far more qualified than her rival.

During his address to the gathering, Rick explained that the council couldn't please everybody on the island. He said,

> There have been complaints made — not to me, as they should be — about the use of the community boat. Some people like to take it out fishing. Nothing wrong in that as long as they look after it and return it in a clean condition to its proper place. I think the problem arises when someone would like the boat on a certain day but, on that particular day, somebody else already had taken it out. This is yet another example of the lack of communication, not only with the council, but between ourselves. We *must* have communication. Nobody knows that better than Bill Rosser. I will now ask Bill Rosser to address this meeting.

Now I hate speaking publicly; I start to shake and any notes I might be holding become impossible to read because they tremble so much. It's not that I'm scared or nervous. Perhaps it's those hundreds of pairs of eyes zooming in on me. Anyway, I made my way to the front and began speaking, shakily at first. I sought out the friendliest eyes and began:

> Mr Chairman, Councillors, brothers and sisters and children: Thank you for allowing me the opportunity to speak to you. The last time I addressed a meeting here on Palm Island was back in 1974. That was the year of the proposed Townsville Takeover bid. They were the days when the Townsville City Council was going to come over here with bulldozers and flatten our community and build a tourist resort. Do you remember? They were going to put in bitumen roads, bulldoze the houses down and place a lot of Palm Island people on to other reserves and keep just a few here to be servants to the white tourists. I know a lot of you people here today remember that battle we had: Bill Congoo, Edith Lenoy, Coster, Aba Johnstone.
>
> The Townsville Takeover was defeated because the then Chairman, the late Fred Clay, fostered and encouraged unity among us here. Fred called meetings and we gave each other strength at those meetings, but it was still difficult to get people to talk about their fears. I suppose one of the strongest of those men was Bill Congoo. He urged people to talk, but they still wouldn't. He said to them, 'Come on, all you people that run the council down, come out here and say what you like'. But still nobody came to talk. Bill said, 'Are you gutless; or what?' And then the people came and had their say. It turned out to be a successful meeting.
>
> Don't forget, back in 1974 white people collected and counted the money from the bar. Now black people are doing it! Remember, back in 1974 white people told us where we could drink, what we could drink and when we could drink. When I first came to Palm Island we were allowed only two cans of beer, opened cans of beer at that! Fred Clay put this up to six cans of unopened beer. He defied the Queensland *Aborigines Act*. It was due to the courage and leadership of Fred Clay that we beat the

Townsville Takeover. He taught us how to be united. We won *because we were united*. Don't think that because the Queensland *Aborigines Act* is abolished that our troubles are over. Sure, the roads have been updated, sewerage has been installed; we are bringing tourists over here under our own private scheme. But watch it! If some tourist operator sees a chance to exploit the tourist industry on Palm Island, there is no way in the world you will stop him! You cannot stop a white man's greed.

I spoke for about ten minutes more, reminding them about how things used to be and how we overcame those adversities. I was lucky enough to have their full attention, mainly, I suspect, because of the nostalgia brought about by my words. But I wanted to exhibit something more than mere words. To this end, I held up a single match and snapped it.

'See how easily I broke that match?'

Most of the meeting nodded. Then I took out the full contents of the box and held them aloft, trying desperately, but in vain, to snap the thick bundle.

'These sticks represent all you people in unity. Singly, you will be smashed easily, like that matchstick; combined and united, like this bundle of matchsticks, you would be strong — unbreakable!'

My exhibition had a sobering effect on the people at the meeting. There was much nodding of heads and humming. I thanked the audience for their attention and handed the floor back to the chairman. There was much more I would have liked to say. A certain religious order, for example, had the kids doing bark paintings, most of them very good examples and the genuine thing. The religious order bought the materials, which was only paint, and the kids provided their own bark. From memory, I think the kids were paid 50 cents each for their paintings and the order sold them on the mainland for $40. Was that good business ... or exploitation?

The meeting broke up at about 5 pm and I headed off home to cadge a cup of tea. The sky was heavily overcast again and the light was fading. As I walked past a small bushy tree which grew beside the road, something caught my eye. It was just a small, quick movement from near the tree. I didn't take much notice of it; it could have been a small animal scurrying for safety on hearing me approach. But when I was about three paces past the bush, I suddenly realised that it was not a small animal: it was, in fact, a squatting Aborigine, and in his hand there glinted the wicked blade of an axe. He wore only a pair of ragged blue denims which had been cut off, or ripped off, at the thighs.

His hair was long and ruffled and a heavy growth of untidy beard gave him the appearance of a troglodyte! At my approach, his eyes narrowed and fixed themselves upon me; his lips turned up in a curl as I stared directly into his eyes. If you show fear in such a situation, you're in trouble. Well, I certainly *felt* fear. I was hoping that he couldn't smell it, as they reckon some animals can. Trying to keep the wobble out of my legs and the hair on my neck from bristling, I took a step towards him.

'What the fucking hell are you doing there?' I demanded. 'You make one move towards me and I'll plant that fucking axe right through your ugly skull.'

I then proceeded to hand him a string of invective such as I had never delivered before. Spurred on by the new strength my abusive voice had generated, I ventured another step towards him and, as I did so, I put my hand behind me in a threatening move, as if I were removing a weapon from behind my back. I hoped this move would cause my aggressor to think twice before launching an attack on me. It worked. The miscreant jumped around, still in a frog-like squatting position, and fled up into the thick edges of the Palm Island scrub. Thank Christ! If my sham — bravado, stupidity, call it what you like — had not worked, I would have had a one-sided battle on my hands. As he disappeared into the bushes, I wondered if he could have been one of those Kadaitcha fellows out for practice!

I had had a similar experience when I was on Palm Island in 1974. On that occasion I was living in a caravan parked beside the old community hall (since burnt down) when a knock came upon the door. When I opened it, the head of a tommyaxe was thrust through the doorway at me. I grabbed the wrist and smashed it against the door jamb. My action failed to dislodge the weapon and my assailant leapt into the van, brandishing the axe above his head. He was absolutely crazed with drink, probably methylated spirits, and I couldn't see the colour of his eyes, only the whites showed. I had no trouble in disarming him and pushing him out of the van, where he fell flat on his buttocks. His head bounced back to such an extent that I thought his neck must surely break. Of course, during the melee, quite a lot of shouting, mainly by me, took place, and a large audience gathered outside. Naturally, I was still trembling but I didn't need to change my clothing! One of the spectators moved over to the form of the moaning attacker and gave his head a rough shove with his boot.

'Ah, it's that Hector,' one of the spectators exclaimed. 'That f'la get killed one day — you see.' I didn't know the man lying on the ground and I didn't particularly want to know him. I have no idea why he would want to attack me. But he was mad with the drink and who knows what went through his mind. Perhaps, during an attack of DTs, he might have imagined — who knows?

(There is a sad sequel to this segment of narrative; the prediction of the spectator finally came true. My would-be assailant was later knifed during an affray on Palm Island and died before he reached the hospital.)

Chapter 14

For the next few days I settled down to some serious work; my notebook and my tapes were flowing over with the results of my talks and interviews with various people on Palm Island. As I was finishing off the last of my notes one afternoon, an old man walked up casually and watched, fascinated, as I fingered the typewriter keys. His curiosity got the better of him, as I knew it would, and he nodded towards the pile of neatly stacked typewritten paper.

'What you do?' he asked me.

I wondered for a while if he would understand, even if I told him.

'Typing,' I told him. 'Making a story.'

He was most impressed and asked me if I could 'make one of them stories' for him. I told him that it might be possible and asked him his name. Before replying, he folded his thin legs and squatted down in front of me.

'My name Harry,' he croaked.

I looked at him fully for the first time: he was tall and thin, a typical stockman. His face wore a day's growth of silver-white beard, and his hair was the same colour, yet quite thick and curly. His face was narrow and his nose seemed to be stuck onto his face as an afterthought. He had piercing black eyes which peered out below thin eyebrows. His shirt was a faded check creation which appeared to be the cast-off of a much larger man as it flowed loosely around his hips. His feet were shod in an old and cracked pair of black shoes which were much too large for him. He wore a tight-fitting pair of brown trousers held up by a piece of plastic rope.

'You lived here long?' I asked him, wondering if he could help me refill my notebook.

'Oh, long time,' he replied, 'since little fella.'

'Where did you come from, Harry?'

'I not know dat,' he admitted. 'I come with my farder. He sent here, long time.'

'Who sent him?'

'Them f'las.' He waved an arm towards the mainland, obviously indicating a great distance.

'You know why he was sent here?' I asked.

'Oh, not know dat,' he answered, shaking his head. 'But one f'la dat knew my farder say he 'it some other f'la. 'it 'im with big stick.'

'Did he tell you why he hit him with a stick?'

'Oh, something 'bout cattle,' he replied, vaguely. 'My farder leave cattle get away, I t'ink.'

'Get away? Was he mustering them and let them break? Is that what you mean?'

He nodded his head at my educated guess: I have heard of many instances where an Aboriginal stockman was flogged because he had let the cattle get away and make a rush back into the bush.

'And your father hit him back with a stick? Is that what happened?' He nodded again.

'I t'ink so. Dat what 'appen,' Harry replied. 'He s'posed to keep 'em goin' round.'

'What do you mean, Harry, "going around"?'

'Well, if you keep 'em goin' round, dey just go round in a ring,' Harry explained. 'If dey stop going round, dey run straight and run away to bush.'

'I see,' I said, 'they broke?' He nodded again; Harry seemed to be a very tired man.

The light was beginning to fade and, as I had just about finished my work, I offered to take Harry to the pub for a beer. He declined and rose from his squatting position. Probably realising that I wanted to put my paperwork away, he walked a few steps away from me and stretched his back.

'I go now, I t'ink,' he said. 'I go 'ome.' He slowly walked up towards the shopping centre and disappeared between the two buildings.

After packing my precious typewritten pages away safely, I decided to go down and share a cup of tea with old Dot. She was always good for a cup of tea and a yarn. And I was anxious to learn of any further adventures she might have had as a station cook in the 'early days', as she called it.

It was just on dark as I knocked on Dot's door.

'You must have smelt it,' she laughed, as she welcomed me inside. 'I've just made a cuppa. Want one?'

'What do you think I came here for?' I jested. She smiled again as she reached up and removed another cup from the shelf. I sat in the same chair I had occupied during my last visit, and Dot placed the cup of steaming tea in front of me.

'How did you go in the city?' she enquired.

'Ah, still a ratrace,' I complained. 'I was glad to get out of the place.' I told her everything of interest that had happened. I was tempted to tell her about our community meeting but I thought better of it. If she had been interested, she would have been there, I thought. 'About the most exciting thing I saw down there was a house on fire.'

She gave a short, sharp laugh and shook her head.

'Ah.' She lifted her head quickly. So quickly, in fact, that she spilt her tea. 'Ah,' she said, 'that reminds me of the time on another station when the kitchen caught fire.'

I settled further into my chair because when Dot starts reminiscing she takes a bit of shutting up. (That is not meant to be disrespectful: I have the greatest respect for people like Dot. If it weren't for them, accounts of Aboriginal history would be very vague indeed.)

'What happened?' I prompted.

That was all dear old Dot needed: 'I was cooking and one day the owner came galloping up to the kitchen and I yelled, "Whoopee!" He said, "Whoopee, be buggered! The bloody house is on fire" I looked up and there was smoke pouring from the roof. He raced into the kitchen and, as he did so, the ceiling fell in on him. He was on fire. I tried to undo the hook that held his pants up so I could take them off; they were smoking at the seams. As I turned him around to get at the hook, a great piece of flesh came away from his back; it just fell away. We did what we could for him until we got him to the Julia Creek Hospital. He had a hard time of it and he died three days' later. His poor wife had just recently died on the train on the way up here.' Dot lowered her head and stared at the floor and I knew that visions of those tragic days had jumped into her mind. I felt a little guilty.

'The entire building burned down,' Dot picked up her story. 'The agents contacted me later and asked me if I would camp in the shearers' quarters until other arrangements could be made. They told me to buy whatever I wanted, so I had a day in town shopping — you know, pots, pans, that sort of thing.'

'Did your belongings get burnt, too?'

'Yes, the whole bloody lot! I had to wear some of the men's clothes for a while. Everything went. All I could save was the old corella; it was about twelve years old. It used to talk real well too. It would say, "Get away-back; get away-back; get away-back". The poor dogs didn't know what to do. They raced around the house looking for cattle.' She laughed at the memory.

'What year would that have been, Dot? When you had the fire, I mean?'

She rubbed her chin with her fingers. 'That would have been in 1959.' She remained silent for a while, her thoughts miles away. 'A fire is so final, isn't it?' she remarked.

'What caused the fire, Dot?' I asked.

'It must have been smouldering in the ceiling for a while,' she replied. 'See, the electrical wiring burned out and that caused the fire. We didn't have generators there; we had electricity. That's what the insurance assessors said anyway.' Dot began to laugh softly as another memory came flooding back.

'There was this mob of sheep there,' she explained. 'It wasn't a big mob. They were along the side of the house and we thought they might get burnt — sheep are silly bloody things, you know. Anyway, we had to chase these sheep out but the only way we could do it was with the truck. But they were frightened of the truck, see. There was a lad there, about nineteen. Well, he was a useless bloody kid! He was sent out there because he was mixed up in some rape or something in Townsville. The others got time and the politicians kicked up a fuss, so the case was reopened and the rapists got a much longer sentence. This useless kid wanted to drive the truck and I told him that he wasn't allowed to drive. I told him to get the dogs working, but they wouldn't work for him. I got in the truck and herded them towards the gate and just as they got there' — Dot looked horrified — 'they were going to break; so I backed the truck into them. Luckily, one went through the gate and, of course, once one goes through, the lot will follow him. They were safe then. This useless lad was getting paid full ringer's wages but he didn't have a clue about anything.' Dot shook her head at the thought of the 'useless' lad.

'What happened after that, Dot?'

'Well, we went into McKinlay to buy new things for the station. I bought what I needed and I was ready to go home; but these two I had brought with me were sitting on the verandah of the pub, drinking beer. Well, I waited and waited for them. I thought, "Bugger this!" So, off I went. I was quite happy driving alone. I'd gone about half a mile, I suppose, when I had to stop and open a gate. When I got to the gate I was grabbed by this bloke. See,' she explained, 'when I took off with the truck, these two jokers followed me. They were shitty because I took off and left them there. This bloke spun me around and abused me.

The language! He called me for everything. I didn't know it at the time but the big bloke — this useless one's mate — was the brother of one of the rapists who got fifteen years' jail!' The simulated fear that Dot had shown during her narrative gave way to a smile. 'I got home alright,' she continued. 'They were just too drunk to catch me.'

It occurred to me that Dot might have been a bit lucky that day. Drunken men sometimes do things that they wouldn't normally do. Nevertheless, I smiled to myself as I pictured Dot dressed in oversized men's shorts and shirt — a sight, I felt sure, that would have done nothing to stir the imaginations or the passions of the two drunken men.

'There was always grog on the place,' Dot told me. 'The station agents used to send it up, and nearly every night there would be a drinking spree in progress. I remember one night in particular: these jokers were getting stuck into the beer when all of a sudden, a shot rang out, then another!' As she reminisced, fear again showed in Dot's face, or was it mystery? She knew I was hanging on her every word.

'Well,' she continued, 'the next thing I heard were footsteps running like the devil. First of all I thought they had shot a snake — snakes were bad there — but this fellow had shot at one of the other drinkers. They were mad with drink! The bloke with the rifle came running around the corner; he said to me, "You get going!" Then he called me all sorts of things. Well,' Dot sat upright, a scared look in her eye, 'I didn't need a second invitation. I grabbed my dog [Bootie] and the waterbag and just took off.'

Notwithstanding the gravity of Dot's situation, I burst out laughing: not at the situation in which she found herself, but at her choice of words. I could well understand that she hadn't needed a second invitation. In my mind's eye I could see a picture of this woman, dressed in outsized clothing, scooting across the paddock with her pet dog tucked firmly under her arm and her hair streaming out behind her. Dot realised the humour of the situation and went into fits of laughter.

'So, off I went,' Dot continued, after composing herself. 'I walked until I was three miles from the road and I could see a car's headlights coming from the direction of Julia Creek. I started to run and I yelled and yelled, but the driver didn't hear me. So I had to walk twenty miles and I had these silly white sandals on and they got full of dirt: it wasn't long before my feet were full of blisters. I had a small handkerchief so I tore it up and wrapped my feet up to stop the bleeding.' She stopped for a moment, looking down at the floor.

'I could see the morning star, so I knew it must be about four o'clock. I wanted to get into McKinlay before daybreak because I was dirty and in a real mess. Now, there was a truck coming towards me. He pulled up and he said, "What the bloody hell is going on here?" I burst into tears. I'm not a crying woman; I'll stand up and fight! Bootie got a set on him. He said, "Come on, get in the truck". Well, I stopped crying and got into the truck and, oooahh!' Dot's face was covered with a painful expression. 'I sat fair on this sharp bloody wool hook.' She half rose from her chair, lifting one buttock at some imaginary pain. 'As though I didn't have enough troubles. Gerry, the driver, tried to get the hook out and all the time Bootie was snapping at him.' Loud laughter filled Dot's house once more as she acted out the process by which the wool hook was finally removed from her bottom. 'Anyway, I got into the police station and I couldn't talk.'

Even though the events she was describing had taken place more than thirty years earlier, Dot had difficulty restraining her emotions. Obviously the shock of the drunken gunman and the ensuing drama, and her long, painful walk, had completely exhausted her.

'Remember me telling you about that car I tried to stop?' Dot continued. 'Well, it was the policeman. His wife had just had a baby and that was the night he brought his wife and the baby home. Of course, when I arrived at his place, he had just gone to sleep. They woke him up and he said, "What's happened?" Old Gerry said, "I don't know. I picked her up in the scrub out there". Then I started bawling out loud. The copper took my hand and stroked it, trying to soothe me. The copper's wife came out to see what all the bawling was about.' Dot looked down bashfully. 'Apparently when I bawl, I've got a loud voice and the more this policeman stroked my hand, the louder I'd howl.' More peals of laughter followed.

'They didn't toss you in the lockup, did they?' I asked, playfully. 'That might have shut you up.'

'No,' she replied, still laughing. 'They treated me real well. It's not every day, or should I say night, that they find a woman lurking in the scrub.'

'How old were you when all this happened?' I asked.

'Oh, I was in my mid-fifties,' she answered frankly.

'Sister Hawke was sent for and as soon as she saw me, she recognised me. By this time, I couldn't walk. Once my feet and legs relaxed, I was buggered.'

'That wool hook in your backside wouldn't have helped either,' I remarked.

'You can say that again,' she said, lifting her bottom off the chair again. 'But that was in my behind; it was nothing to what my poor blistered feet were going through. But anyway, I told the police about the shots I had heard back on the station and how he had menaced me with the rifle. Of course, the state I was in made him think that I was imagining the whole thing. I told him that I certainly was *not* imagining it and that a man *was* running — *fast!*'

By this time the ashtray was full to the top with the butts of cigarettes we'd smoked during the excitement of her storytelling. Noticing this, Dot jumped up with surprising agility and emptied it. She made more tea for herself and a cup of coffee for me and returned once more to her chair.

'Well,' she continued, stirring her tea, 'Sister Hawke had bandaged my feet and they were feeling much better so we all took off for the station. When we arrived I found that they had let all my tyres down. The poor policeman had to — ' She couldn't finish the sentence: she had burst out into uncontrollable laughter. Although I had no idea what had caused the outburst, I joined in her laughter. There we were, both laughing our silly heads off, and only one of us knew what the bloody hell we were laughing at! Dot finally got herself together and wiped her eyes.

'That poor copper,' she began to explain, 'here he was, he had just finished running backwards and forwards to the hospital in Julia Creek for the last week; he brings the kid home — it hasn't stopped bawling since — and he's buggered for want of sleep; and just as he gets to sleep, I come in, bawling my eyes out. So out he comes and, in the boiling sun, he has to pump up four tyres. Then he had to investigate to see whether this fellow was still alive; they both were, these two hoons. He found the spent cartridge cases and he said it appeared that more shots had been fired after I left. I didn't hear them because I was too busy running.' She stopped talking and sipped her tea.

I looked at Dot with mixed feelings. I was pleased that I hadn't lived through some of her experiences; yet in a way I envied her. I envied her lifestyle: the excitement, and the challenges she had had to face. Dot could sit and talk about the old times and not repeat herself once.

'I spent that Christmas in hospital.' Dot was speaking again. 'While I was there, they brought a fellow in; he had been out mustering and his horse caught him up against a snapped-off limb of a log and cut his leg off.' I must have swallowed hard and changed colour because Dot gave me a look that made me ashamed of being so weak-gutted. I looked back at her and shrugged. I weakly defended myself by telling her that it wasn't every day someone told me that someone got their leg cut off.

Dot ignored my explanation. 'It was cut off at the knee: they had to bring in the Flying Doctor. It was only hanging by a thread.' I held my cup to my lips in an effort to conceal my horror at the picture my fertile imagination had conjured up. 'They were short-staffed and I had to help by cleaning things, rolling up cotton wool. Things like that. We had a nice Christmas in that hospital.' I said nothing.

'Of course, they hadn't paid me — the firm — and I was broke. I asked the Matron if I could ring my daughter in Adelaide, reverse charge. She told me I could but then — ' She broke off, and spread her hands on the table to convey her feeling of despair. 'But I'd lost my glasses. I lost them in the fire when the house burned down. Well, I'm blind without my glasses so I contacted the agent and asked them to get another pair for me from the opticians — they had the prescription. I didn't even have a pin to hold my dress together. I told them that, and they sent me up a brooch.' Dot laughed at the absurdity. 'It wasn't very practical but it held my dress together.'

'Dot,' I interrupted, 'when you were in Julia Creek Hospital, were there any blacks there?'

She fondled the point of her chin. 'Let me see. That was in 1959. No, there were no blacks there; there wasn't on Legaven station. Only white workers.'

'You had on other stations though, didn't you?' I changed the subject, anxious to get her mind off that hospital.

'Oh, yes,' she replied. 'When I was on Wondoola, Lorraine — the Lorraine station was on the Leichhardt River. It was a big place. I was in contact with blacks on Tobermory station, too. Then there was Thorntonia station. That was the place where I had a blackfellow's axe. One of the people there hounded me because he wanted this bloody axe. "Take it," I told him. He said he wanted it for a paperweight. When I saw old Dick, [a black worker], I asked him if he ever saw any blackfellow's axes around. He said, "You-i," and he came back with half a dozen of the things. He told me about when he was a little boy — he was an old man when I knew him — how the policemen would come down and shoot them. He was one of the blacks who escaped. The blacks lived on the river but they were nearly all killed. The squatters used to ride up with the police too.' She raised her voice as she spoke. 'It wasn't only the police.'

'Yes, I know,' I replied. 'It was in the squatters' interests to get rid of the blacks. They shot them by the thousands.'

'That's right,' Dot agreed. 'And the squatters wanted to be in on the kill too. Old Dick almost had tears in his eyes as he was telling me about this massacre. See, they were all related. Dick tried to explain this cousin-brother thing but I could never get the hang of it.'

'Well,' I replied, 'it's really quite simple. A cousin-brother is a person who has the same mother but a different father or vice versa.'

'Oh, I see,' Dot opened her eyes wide in understanding. 'It really is simple, isn't it?'

'Yes. Actually, to simplify it further, a cousin-brother is a half-brother.'

'Old Dick was quite emotional when he was telling me the story. He just had his arms limp by his sides as he told me about it. My dog, Bootie, followed Dick like a shadow. I will never forget the day he and Bootie went down to the windmill. A great big buffalo came around looking for a drink. Now Dick had never seen a buffalo before. That buffalo had strayed from the Northern Territory. Whether the buffalo made a noise or not I don't know, but the two of them came running into the kitchen, completely out of breath. Old Dick was nearly white with fright. They didn't leave the kitchen for the rest of the day. When the boss came home, he shot it. They are very destructive on fences; they just walk straight through.'

'You mentioned before that you worked on Tobermory station. How long were you there?' I asked her.

'Not for long,' she replied, 'but I was there when they told me about the "hanging tree". The man that told me was such a truthful man. He wouldn't tell a story unless it was absolutely true. See, it was great fun for the whites to run the blacks down and shoot them. They couldn't ride with the hounds here, like they did in England, so they hunted blacks instead, just like they hunted the foxes in England.'

'Dot,' I enquired, 'what pay did you receive for station cooking?'

'It varied from place to place,' she replied. 'The average pay would be about ten shillings a week.'

'Wasn't much, was it?' I remarked.

'Oh, I got along,' she replied. 'What I didn't like out there were the dust storms. I remember talking to a man one morning and he told me that there was going to be a terrible dust storm that day. Well, that afternoon he came riding up and I said to him, "Where's that big dust storm you were talking about?" He said, "Look behind you, girl". I turned around and there was this terrible big wall of dust coming towards us. It was as high as a mountain. We all got under the tables with towels and buckets of water to filter the dust so we could breathe. Those dust clouds are frightening. They are red and black and purple and they come in fast. During the storm I could hear "ping, ping, ping". I thought it was raining but it was stones. The wind was so strong that it lifted little stones and pelted them onto the roof. It knocked out all the power. We were in the dark until we lit the Millars lamps. Have you ever seen them?' she asked.

'Yes, I have,' I replied.

The lamp she referred to was beautifully shaped, with a fuel tank at the top of the thick supporting stem, usually made of glass. This tank was filled with paraffin oil. The wick was circular, and was controlled by a small adjusting wheel at the side. The glass lampshade, called the 'glass', acted as the chimney: it was tall and elegant, narrow at the top and widening out towards the bottom, which fitted neatly onto the top of the fuel tank. Covering this glass was another, more bulbous globe, usually with a frosted effect. It was this finish that gave it its soft light, not at all like that from the old kerosene lamp. The outer rim of the lamp was decorated with delicate filigree work: it looked like silver lacework. But the most interesting feature was the series of small, evenly spaced holes around its base and it was through these holes that the light drew its oxygen. It wouldn't matter how expertly the wick was trimmed, if those holes were blocked the lamp couldn't function satisfactorily.

'I'll never forget that man who warned me of the dust storm.' Dot began yet another story from her past. 'He owned one of the stations I worked on. He used to like reading these Deadwood Dicks. He had a tea-chest full of them beside his bed (it was only an old camp-stretcher). He wasn't a poor man; the station was worth three hundred and fifty thousand pounds. This was in 1960. Anyway, one day a hen came in and made a nest in this box of cowboy books. It eventually laid an egg in it and eventually it hatched out a chicken.'

'One chicken?'

'Yes, it only had one egg. The trouble was, the sand in the yard was too hot for it, so it lived inside the house for months. It became the house pet.' She smiled at her memories, but soon her smile gave way to a frown, creating uncharacteristic furrows on her brow. Her eyes darted from the floor to me and back several times. I could tell that some unpleasant memory — some bad experience from her distant past — was troubling her.

'One owner,' she began, 'he must have been married before because he had a girl, his daughter. I don't know what age she was. This day she went out mustering cattle and the horse came back with its reins trailing. It was just at dusk and it was too late for the men to backtrack, but they did ride out and followed the path of the incoming cattle. That was easy to do because they leave behind a trail of — well, you know what! They lit fires everywhere and they cooeed all night.'

She gave a deep sigh; her tale was obviously causing her some distress. 'Around about nine o'clock that morning they found her: she was sitting up against a tree, dead.' Dot stopped speaking again and lowered her eyes. It was quite obvious that in her mind's eye she was reliving that tragic event. 'She was just leaning up against the tree with the most horrible look on her face; absolute terror. They rang the doctor and when he examined her he said she had died of fright: there was sheer terror on her face.'

'What would have frightened her to that extent?' I enquired. 'She must have been used to the bush.'

'Oh, some sound,' Dot guessed. 'She might have heard a noise she did not recognise and might have seen — or thought she saw — something horrible that was not really there. I don't know.' She thought about it for a while, slowly shaking her head from time to time.

'Of course, bush people are so good at telling ghost stories,' she said. 'Those ghastly ghost tales! She had been around camp fires when that sort of talk was going on. She could have imagined anything.'

'Difficult to believe, isn't it?'

'It certainly is,' Dot replied. 'They held a post-mortem on her but there wasn't a mark on her body. They don't know how she died. All they could find were her tracks going around and around the tree. She was a good little rider and they think she must have got off her horse to go to the toilet. Her father never really got over that.'

'The horse came home by itself?'

'Yes. It was the sort of horse that would have followed the cattle. Because of the dust, no one saw the reins trailing. When they *did* notice, it was too late; you've got no hope of finding anyone in that bush at night.'

She sipped her tea thoughtfully for a while, then, carefully replacing her cup upon the table, she turned to me once more.

'I must say that since I came back to Palm Island I've had plenty of time to think,' she remarked. 'It's so lovely and quiet down this neck of the woods.'

'It's a bit rowdier up near the pub,' I remarked. 'It's a wonder to me how some of those blokes get home without falling off the side of the road.'

'Yes,' Dot agreed, 'it's a wonder they don't cripple themselves, the way they fall all over the place.'

As she stopped speaking, her face took on a strange look and she rubbed the tip of her nose with her thumb. She was obviously in deep thought once more.

'Talking about crippled blackfellows,' she began, 'there were seven boys on the station; one of them was crippled. The owner's wife didn't take to them at all. Now, this woman could swear like a bullock driver and this particular morning she had a go-in with one of them. As you know, Bill, the biggest insult a blackfellow can hand out to a white person is to point his bare backside at them. I was just in time to see this bloke drop his pants, turn around and bend over. Anyway, to get back to this crippled boy; he wasn't accepted at all. He was accepted by the blacks but not by the whites. He'd be about fourteen, I suppose. He'd had polio. Anyway, the boss — he was a big, raw-boned man — said to this crippled boy, "Get up on that horse". Well, this horse could really buck and the kid said, "No". Well,' Dot drew up her shoulders to full height, 'for a black to say "No" to a white man! It's unheard of. The boss had his stockwhip with him. I'd forgotten about my cooking; I wanted to see what was going on. Well, the mother of the boy, a big, rough-looking woman, went out and stood in front of the boss because she was not going to let him hit her crippled child. I could see what would happen so I ran out and stood in front of *her*. I said to him, "Don't you hit *me!*" He was flicking the whip around and the old bookkeeper — he was only about five foot two [155 cm] — came out with a feather duster. He trained all those kids with a feather duster. He said, "Put that whip down and ride that bloody horse yourself". You could see the owner wilting and the bookkeeper made him get up onto the horse. It wasn't long before he was thrown off. He wanted this kid to take the friskiness out of the horse. Poor little devil, he wouldn't have been able to ride that horse even if he'd had two good legs.' Dot had told me earlier that his wife had died on the train and I was tempted to ask her if she knew how the woman had died. But, when I reflected, I was loath to have her recall more bad memories, and I let the question die on my lips.

A knock came on the door. Dot rose and opened it and was confronted by two young ladies who were trying to sell Bibles. Dot declined their offer gracefully and told them, in her own inimitable way, that she already had seven Bibles, 'one for each day of the week'. As they left, I could sense Dot's inward smile. She was a true bush wag. She settled back into her chair and resumed her narrative.

'One owner and I used to swap reading material,' she told me as she stirred a fresh cup of tea. 'I'll never forget the day a woman named Betty kept pestering me about another woman named Winnie George being arrested for murdering her baby. She'd been raped, see. When the baby was six days old, Winnie George knocked it on the head. I said to this Betty, "It's murder and you can't do anything about it". She said to me, "You do something about it!" So eventually I went up to the owner and told him about it. He said, "Bloody murder. Let her get on with her work". I told him that Winnie and this Betty were cousins. "They're *all* bloody cousins!" he said.

'Was this woman really arrested for murder?' I asked her.

'Oh, yes,' Dot affirmed. 'Her husband, Ned, worked on the station where Winnie George was raped. The manager of the station had a brother and he was a real fiend. This swine used to walk up every Saturday night to where the gins were camped to have sexual relations — it was downright bloody rape — with the gins. He said that if he was ever charged with rape his defence would be the gins wanted "baccy" and traded him for it. Not only was it *his* defence, it was every white man's defence. If an Aboriginal girl complained to the police, she would get kicked down the steps! That was at Camooweal. No white man, no matter what he did, would ever be arrested because all they had to say was "she wanted baccy and I exchanged her baccy for sex".' Dot's lips thinned in an expression of contempt, and her eyes showed her disgust.

She seemed anxious to explain the rape and the subsequent killing of the baby. I waited for her to continue. 'See, Winnie George's husband, Ned, knew all about windmills and this overseer took him away out in the bush and left him there to look after the windmills. He took out tucker and there was a shed there and the overseer left him there for months. He only took him away from the camp so he could get at Winnie. He just used her up.'

'Wasn't the station manager awake-up to what was going on?' I asked. 'I mean, surely someone knew.'

'Of course they knew,' Dot replied, hotly. 'They didn't care. She was only a black gin. When the baby was born she didn't tell Ned because he would have belted her around the ears; so when the murder occurred, Winnie was put in jail and Ned continued on at the station.'

'When did this all take place, Dot?' I asked her. 'Do you remember what year that was?'

'Yes,' Dot replied immediately, 'it was 1963. I got to know the priest there and I asked him if he could do anything for Winnie George. I asked him if he could get her out of jail. He said, "Missus, it was murder. She really killed that baby, you know". I told him that in her eyes it was tribal law she was carrying out. Now, Bill, I don't know what he did, but she was taken to Rockhampton and charged with murder. Now if she had been convicted, she would have been sent to Palm Island and she would never have seen her children again. I know for a fact that, when black women become an embarrassment, they are brought here to Palm Island on some trumped-up charge. I know one woman who was brought here to Palm Island because she became an embarrassment to a manager at Normanton; she was having her fourth child to him. He just had her sent to Palm Island. She hadn't done anything other than sleep with him.' Dot looked at me through narrowed eyes; her breathing was heavy and her jaw set in that now-familiar look of disgust.

'When Winnie George came up for trial, the case was read out and the judge said, "Case dismissed". Winnie just walked out of the court; she didn't say goodbye or kiss my foot. She just couldn't get back to Camooweal quickly enough. One white woman at Camooweal said, "I wouldn't have her near the place", and it wasn't until some time later that I found out that she was the sister-in-law of the rapist . . . When she got back to the station, she wasn't allowed to stay but old Ned was . . . I left and went to Brisbane. I never went west again.'

A sad look crossed Dot's face as she stopped speaking and her eyes moistened. She lowered her head and gazed blankly at the floor. I tried to think of something to say that might take her mind off whatever was causing her such sadness. There are times in the life of an oral historian when the probing, however gentle or tactful it might be, causes pain to the person being questioned as some long-forgotten memory surfaces. This was obviously one of those times and I intimated that it was time to finish. But Dot was made of sterner stuff, and wanted to continue. I respectfully declined, however, and got up to leave.

By the time I walked up the stairs of Assam's house it was about 4.30 pm. Henry was there, sprawled out on the floor with his head only inches from a screaming tape-recorder. The noise was deafening.

'Jesus Christ!' I chided. 'What the bloody hell is *that*?'

'Aw, Slade,' Henry replied. 'Good, eh?' I put on my best look of disgust.

'I'll play you a real tape later,' I promised him.

'Yair? What is it? Rock and roll?'

'No,' I replied, sedately. 'It's called "We'll Gather Lilacs". '

'We'll gather *what*?'

'Lilacs,' I told him again. 'You wait till you hear it; you'll want to listen to it all night.' I smiled to myself. I didn't imagine for one moment that Henry would have the vaguest appreciation of Richard Tauber's rendition of the ballad from *Perchance to Dream*; but it would be fun, I thought, to watch his reaction. I don't suppose Henry even knew what a tenor was. I found the tape and, when that ghastly Slade tape ended, I put my cassette into the machine and switched it on. Soon the golden voice of Richard Tauber floated across the room. Henry looked at the recorder and then with a frown, 'What the fuck's *that?*' he asked incredulously.

'There, you see,' I chided him, 'you don't appreciate good music.' Henry listened until the tape ended.

'There, wasn't that terrific?' I teased him.

'Aw *fuck!*' he expostulated. I couldn't help laughing at his disgust.

'Would you like to hear some more?' I teased him.

'Stick it in your arse!' he laughed. 'Don't play any more.'

At this point, Assam's car roared up the road. He bounded up the steps and sat down heavily on the floor of the verandah. He was furious. His windscreen had been smashed again.

'That's the third windscreen that's been broken now,' he complained.

Henry went inside and brought out a stubby of beer and handed it to Assam with brotherly understanding. Assam took a deep swallow. Before long the conversation had turned to some shapely females who had arrived on the island. The windscreen was soon forgotten!

Chapter 15

I awoke next morning to a glorious sunny day. A gentle sea breeze was playing with the fronds of the coconut palms. The leaves of the wild plum trees were still wet with dew and as the breeze caught them, the sun turned the dew drops into golden sequins. Children were already playing on the beach; still more were walking slowly along the road, examining the sides for any folding money inebriates might have dropped the previous night during their drunken staggering home. I didn't like their chances: scroungers, who were much more cunning than the kids, would already have scoured the area. When I walked into the kitchen, I found Delphine sitting at the table, a book in front of her and a steaming cup of coffee beside her. She looked up as I entered.

'How's the tea?' I asked her.

'Plenty,' she smiled, 'there's a whole potful. I knew you'd be spitting for tea as soon as you woke.' She obviously knew me well. 'You want breakfast?'

'No, thanks, love,' I told her. 'I'm not hungry; but this tea will sure go down well.'

Delphine was a really good woman. Her shiny black hair framed her slightly plump face and her skin was like black, shiny silk. Her eyes, too, were black and limpid. When she looked at you, a tiny gleam appeared in each corner. Her face was well formed, with full lips and a rounded, determined chin. When Delphine smiled, a set of white, perfectly-spaced teeth was revealed. Her face was fashioned in such a way that she seemed to wear a perpetual grin.

Soon Jamie, the catcher of wild bulls, entered and sat down, squeezing his head between his rough, horny hands.

'Oh, my fucking head,' he moaned. He had been on a drinking spree the previous night by all appearances.

'Serves you right,' Delphine was unsympathetic. 'You blokes that go drinking deserve a crook head.'

'Any tea?' he enquired.

Delphine pointed to the stove with her chin.

'There, look,' she said. Jamie poured himself a mug of tea, wincing all the while.

'How many wild bulls are you going to catch today, Jamie?' I asked. 'There's some pink ones down among the coconut trees just waiting for you.'

'Aw, fuck off!' he replied, a smile spreading across his face. I liked Jamie. He was a good sport.

At about 10.30 am I decided to go down to the village to see what was happening: the pub would be open and I knew Bill Congoo would be hovering around close by. I found him sitting on an old oil drum across from the pub.

'G'day, you old bastard,' he greeted me, throwing away a well-chewed cigarette butt. He rose and came towards me; for about the tenth time in two weeks we shook hands.

'Got a smoke?' he asked. I had anticipated his request and my packet of Hallmarks was already in my hand. I held out the packet and he selected one with trembling fingers.

'You cold?' I asked him.

'No,' he replied, 'I need a charge. You got the price?'

Since I expected to leave the island any day now, I decided to shout him a final drink.

'Hang on,' I said. 'Be back soon.' I darted across to the pub and bought a six-pack of Fosters and brought it back across the road. Bill's eyes didn't leave it for a moment. He lifted his head, seemingly trying to smell the beer.

'Let's go down there, Bill,' he suggested, indicating a nice sandy spot on the beach. 'It's nice and sunny there.'

We walked the few yards to the sunny spot and sat on a water pipe. I put the six-pack down but it hadn't had time to collect any sand before Bill picked it up and anxiously twisted a can from its plastic holder. He tore back the aluminium tag and poured the whole contents down his throat in one go.

'Bloody hell, Bill,' I exclaimed, 'you'll kill yourself. You must have been in a bad way.' He nodded to me. His shakes had already stopped and the frown had left his face.

'I was nearly dying,' he said as he wiped the drips from his chin.

'Christ, don't die,' I teased. 'Here, have another one.' He pulled away another can but this time he wasn't quite so desperate. As he sat sipping the new can, old Tommy came across to us, eyes gleaming hopefully.

'Have a beer,' I invited him, saving him the indignity of having to ask.

As he tore one from the pack, four or five young men came across the road and approached us. I tipped immediately from their demeanour that they were smart little bastards. They walked stiff legged and stopped in front of us.

'Hey, you f'la,' the tallest of them addressed Bill, 'gib me a drag on your can.' Bill eyed them closely and clutched his can to his chest.

'Go and get fucked!' he retorted. 'You're not getting my fucking beer! Go on, fuck off!'

One of the others turned to Tommy.

'Hey, old man,' he said, disrespectfully, 'you gib me a drink, eh?' Tommy looked up at the would-be standover merchants with eyes like those of a chastised bloodhound. He was being intimidated and he made to pass his can up to the black lout. I laid a restraining hand on his arm.

'Listen, you mob of thugs,' I said to them, hotly, 'do what Bill told you to do. Go and fuck your boot!' I was in a rage to think that these lairs could come up from the city and carry on like young Humphrey Bogarts. They don't have enough brains, or friends, in the city to feed themselves so they come up to provincial towns and prey on the old and infirm. They're street-blacks, the type who, with their standover and bullying tactics, are responsible for giving blacks a bad name.

'Who you?' the tall one demanded.

'I'm the one who bought the beer,' I told him.

'Well, you gib us some; come on.'

Now, I carry a genuine Waluwarra tribe pointing bone. It was given to me by an old former Kadaitcha man in Dajarra. I carried it as a lucky charm. Some charm!

I put my hand in my inside coat pocket, withdrew the polished emu bone, and let the string unfurl, the bunch of emu feathers dangling at the bottom. Bill and Tommy almost shit themselves at the sight of this powerful hoodoo device. Their eyes opened wide and Bill actually spilled his beer.

'Know what this is?' I held it towards the group of louts. They stared at it and immediately backed off. I gave the bone a quick shake and held it closer to them. It was obvious that they had heard about the terrifying powers of this old Aboriginal 'weapon', no doubt through the tales the old people told. I gave the feathers another shake. That did it: they turned on their heels and fled for dear life, not bothering to look back.

Tommy's eyes were twice their normal size as he backed away from it. 'Put that terrible thing away,' he demanded, shakily. 'Don't you "catch" me!'

Bill, too, was wide-eyed, his mouth half-open as he looked sideways at the dangling brown emu feathers. 'Put it away, Bill,' he pleaded. 'Put the thing away.' Neither of them swore, which showed they had great respect for my lucky charm. I replaced the gleaming white bone in my pocket and smiled after the still-fleeing youths. Tommy and Bill regained their seats on the water pipe and breathed deeply.

'I haven't seen one of those for a long time,' Tommy said. 'I was "caught" once.'

'What happened?' I asked him. 'Can you tell me about it?'

'Aw, yes,' Tommy replied. I could well understand Tommy's respect for the pointing bone: he was a fullblood and, no doubt, had witnessed the results of its power in tribal lore. He fiddled nervously with his can of beer.

'Well,' he told us, 'I did something wrong, a long time ago.' He looked at me quickly. 'I just forget what it was, now.'

I secretly thought he hadn't forgotten. You don't forget an experience like that.

'This bloke "caught" me and I got sick; I nearly die. Another old bloke knew I was "caught" and he told me he could fix me up.' He had a swig of his beer before continuing. I got the impression he'd need a few more beers after he'd finished telling his story.

'Well, this bloke rolled me on my guts and poked around on my back and, before I knew it, there was blood everywhere. I couldn't feel anything; it didn't hurt at all. Then he sat me up and showed me a little bit of bone — I think it was bone — that he had taken out of my back. The blood was all gone. I stood up and I was better. I don't want that again.'

'Why were you "caught"?' I pried.

'Aw, I forget,' he repeated.

'You lyin' old bastard!' Bill said to him, laughing. 'You wouldn't forget.' Tommy just put his head down and smiled openly.

We finished off the six-pack, then my two companions thanked me for the grog and wandered off towards the pub, probably looking for the 'price' again. I wandered back home and busied myself with my typewriter for the remainder of the day, chronicling the events of the past two days.

Usually when I write I have a few kids around me, watching as the typed words appear magically on the paper, but not this time. I get on very well with kids; I have a great respect for them, and hope for the future generations. Mainly though, I think, I get on well with them because I'm a bit of a kid at heart myself. On my first visit to Palm Island, in 1974, the kids and I walked for miles seeking bush tucker. But those kids have all grown up and many have left the island for better, or worse, things. Some now have kids of their own, some have jobs, and some, unfortunately, are in gaol. In those days I had a large caravan where the kids would visit me every night, and we would yarn on for hours; Palm Island kids weren't renowned for going to bed early. They would delight in having me tell them ghost stories. I would think up something crazy, like a headless man coming down the road. The kids would look down the road, squealing to high heaven, and then, convinced the headless man was about to enter, they would throw themselves under the bed or hide beneath the blankets, their mouths agape in timorous anxiety and their black eyes grown to twice their normal size. I would then end off the story by shouting dramatically, 'Look out! He's coming in the door.' On hearing that, they would all race to me and huddle against me for protection. Their frenzy, however, was always followed by 'Tell us another story, Uncle Bill'. When they tired of that pastime, they would crowd into and over my Ford XP station wagon and we would 'go for a burn' down to the air strip, with kids hanging off the side. The parents would smile and wave.

It is quite possible that they went along with my goings-on only to humour me. I'm sure they thought I was mad. Well, maybe. But I loved those Palm Island kids; I will never forget the countless hours of joy they brought me. And I had been saddened to hear on my return to Palm Island that some of my little friends had died as the result of alcohol. I had tried to reach the kids on my present journey, but they weren't the same somehow: with few exceptions they appeared to have no fun in their lives; the happy laughter no longer echoed throughout the island. Perhaps it was me; perhaps *I* had changed.

As I reminisced, I realised that this was the last full day I would spend on Palm Island. I sought out Moa and his dad, Old Assam, and we shared a jug of beer. Soon we were joined by Henry and Assam Clay, and Jamie. We all sat on the verandah of Assam's house, Delphine joyfully pushing the swing. I don't know how many cigarettes we smoked, but the ashtray was emptied many times as we talked about the old times and what the future might hold. We finally surrendered to the sandman and, one by one, we drifted off to our respective beds.

I woke early the next morning. It was time for me to return to my small flat in Redcliffe. It would be empty and lonely now that my mother was no longer there. I took my luggage and went looking for Bill Congoo. I found him sitting down near the jetty; it appeared he had passed out and remained there all night. His eyes were red and his hands shook.

'Feel like a drink, Bill?' I asked. He shook his head.

'No, fuck the drink,' he said, earnestly. 'I'm going to try and give it away. I'm always fucking crook.'

'Take a lot of guts, Bill,' I told him. 'You've been drinking for a long time. It won't be easy.'

'I ain't got any fuckin' guts,' he said, explosively. He held out his hands. They trembled uncontrollably. 'Look at me!' He lowered his head in shame. Or was it disgust?

'When did you have your last drink, Bill?' I asked.

'Not since yesterday; since you pulled that fuckin' bone out,' he replied, sulkily. 'It's just as well you did, though. Those bastards might've belted the lot of us. They were bad bastards. They might have kicked our guts in.'

'No worries,' I comforted him. 'I'll bet they're still running.'

'I nearly ran, too,' Bill admitted. 'You frightened shit out of me. Old Tommy is still shaking!'

We talked together for a while, until I heard the approach of the aircraft which would take me to Townsville. We shook hands warmly.

'When you coming back?' he asked me.

'I don't know, Bill,' I answered. 'Maybe a year. Who knows? I might be a pisspot myself by then.'

He smiled at my inference, but didn't take offence. He knew he was one, so why worry?

'Next time I see you, you'll be as fat as mud if you stay off the grog,' I told him. He laughed out loud, which was good to hear.

The community bus pulled up alongside, and I stowed my bags into the back; then we headed for the landing strip. Maybe Bill would stay off the grog, I mused. I hoped so. Maybe he would set an example. I hoped so even more.

In many ways this visit to Palm Island had been disappointing. Admittedly I had renewed old friendships, made new friends, and added to my knowledge of Aboriginal suffering through the years. But the revival of the news sheet, the reason for my visit, had not happened. In spite of my efforts, not a single new copy of *Smoke Signal* had appeared. Most disappointing, though, was the worsening alcoholism and violence on the island and the evidence that rescinding Queensland's *Aborigines Act* had not been the magic cure people had expected.

The Aboriginal drinking problem, of course, is not confined to Palm Island, and where it will end no one knows. But for this and the coming generation, it seems the pattern and example have already been set: I have seen kids as young as nine so drunk they can barely move. Increasing numbers of non-Aboriginal children also have this problem, but for them support systems are usually available. For black kids, it's different. For a start most of them can't get sufficient education. Money is not the problem: they are eligible for Aboriginal school grants. No, the problem is racism. In 1991 it still exists. I have known black kids who have tried to paint themselves white, with flour. It would be funny if it weren't so pathetic.

Many Aboriginal people, of course, avoid these problems; some of them are caught up in religious groups. Well, if it takes religion to keep them off the booze, let's go for it! One thing is an absolute certainty: while alcohol is made available on Aboriginal reserves, or 'shires', the advancement of their self-determination, their dignity and their very future is forfeit.

Perhaps I'll be taken to task over these views, but mainly, I suggest, from the street militants, or white hangers-on and do-gooders, none of whom are worth worrying about anyway.

Before I entered the aircraft, I took a long, hard look around. Would I ever be back? I rather thought not. But how can one turn one's back on a lifetime of living: the pathos; the disgust; the ignorance of which white society is capable; the memories.

I looked down onto the receding island from the aircraft. Of course I will be back!

Epilogue

More than three years later, in 1992, arguments continue about the establishment of a tourist resort, and conditions on Palm Island are still far from ideal. Over the years, various leaders on the island have tried to make conditions better for their people, but up till now none, however good their intentions, have succeeded. This is because the seeds of the problem lie so far in the past.

In 1974, Fred Clay gave his all in an endeavour to make life livable, but he and the Palm Island chairpersons who succeeded him were foiled by Queensland's heinous *Aborigines Act*. It was this Act that prevented tribal elders from instructing young Aborigines in the culture and customs of the Aboriginal race. Even further, Aborigines were forbidden, under threat of prison, even to practise these customs, including the initiation ceremonies and corroborees that had been such an important part of the Aboriginal lifestyle. At the same time, they were robbed of other rights, including the right to see their wives or husbands, their children, and their other relatives.

This denial of their culture and rights inexorably caused constraints on black society, leading to forced departure from the land, the loss of socialisation skills, the loss of the kinship system, and the breaking up of families and traditional lifestyles. Aborigines are confused, suffering from overwhelming self-reproach and remorse. Theirs is the legacy of confusion and hopelessness. Many reach the point where they take their own lives, in or out of gaol.

All these effects have been felt on Palm Island, and in spite of the rescinding of the Act are still obvious today. The situation has been made even worse by white society's ignorance of Aboriginal customs. It forced as many as seven different tribes — all with different cultures and customs — to live together on this small island and expected them to co-exist. The friction that already existed between them still exists to a lesser extent today. Even now, white society fails to appreciate that Aborigines don't necessarily react to life's pressures in the way whites themselves would do. Frequently their solution is to resort to alcohol, and there can be no doubt that alcohol abuse has emerged as the greatest threat to Aboriginal society today. The people of Palm Island realise this but are seemingly powerless, or unwilling, to do anything about the problem. For many years in the past I championed the rights of Aborigines to enjoy similar drinking conditions to whites. Now, I know I was wrong, dreadfully wrong! Past Chairman of the Palm Island Aboriginal Council, Tom Geia, has it summed up correctly. In a recent statement to the press, he said:

> Very few people in the wider community really understand how recently we Aboriginals in Queensland emerged from the supervision of the Queensland *Aborigines Act*. The last vestiges of that Act didn't disappear until 1984. That's only seven years ago. What it meant to us to grow up and live under the Act was that we had absolutely no control over our lives.
>
> We did what we were told, went where we were told, married whom we were told to, worked at what we were told to, ate and drank what we were told to ... if you have lived like that for, say, 40 or 50 years, it's very difficult to know how to take control of your own life overnight when the opportunity is finally given to you.
>
> (*Townsville Bulletin* 26 June 1991)

Mr Geia also recognises the health problems on the island and is noted for his disparaging remarks on the poor treatment meted out on the island, maltreatment, he claims, that has been going on for years. I must say, however, that, to my mind, the nursing staff at the hospital were a very dedicated lot during my experiences on Palm Island but, of course, that was in 1974.

There have been others in power on the island who have their hearts, and their heads, in the right place. For instance, past Chairman of the Palm Island Aboriginal Council, Jacob Baira, recognised the problems and where the solution lay. During his term of office, he said: 'The time has come to fight for the younger generation, not for ourselves — that time has gone' (*Townsville Bulletin*, 30 October 1987). He also realises that liquor abuse is a problem.

Who, however, can fail to sympathise with Ricky Clay who, faced with the seeming hopelessness of the situation on Palm Island, stated: 'When we bury our dead, we cry for them and their families. Can you tell me who else cares?' (*Courier-Mail*, 2 September 1988)

Whatever words of wisdom have been spoken by past chairpersons, and however zealous those people may have been, in my opinion the one who has the greatest understanding and zeal is Ms Sylvia Reubens, the current Palm Island Aboriginal Council Chairperson. She recognises *all* the problems: 'Violence, Aboriginal deaths in custody, excessive drinking, health problems — the social life of hopelessness.'

Under her chairmanship, however, a flicker of hope has appeared. A Community Development Employment Program, launched in 1989, has given employment to many people who have never worked before, and as a result domestic violence has lessened. Instead of watching their parents sitting idle or drinking under a tree, children now have a different model to follow. They realise their parents have the ability to work (*Weekend Australian*, 23-24 September 1989).

It is, of course, early days yet, and meanwhile life on Palm Island goes on — the violence, the bashings, the rapes, the murders. And my experience in these matters tells me that white society's justice will never stamp them out. Aborigines must be allowed to try and recapture their culture and traditions, part of which must be the traditional tribal punishment of offenders against their society. White police will never curb black wrongdoers because of the lack of respect blacks have for white police officers. This disrespect goes back to the nineteenth century when white troopers of the Native Mounted Police Force shot, poisoned and bashed to death countless thousands of Aborigines. These tales of horror have been handed down from father to son for generations. Though they may not mention it, most blacks know what happened during those 'early years' of settlement. The hatred is deep-seated, indeed.

Finally, in order to regain their self-esteem, the residents of Palm Island, like blacks throughout Australia, do not need journalists who persist in giving Aborigines bad, racist press. It never ceases to amaze me that some uninspired journalists take delight in writing derogatory articles about blacks. Here is a sample taken from the *Townsville Bulletin* of 11 April 1991. The journalist had spent three nights on Palm Island!

> 'Oh, what a night . . . ' The words of the song echoed out to sea as two women stood face to face screaming obscenities. Suddenly the drunken shouting exploded into flailing arms and legs as the two attacked each other . . . one of the combatants retreated into the crowd . . . trying to shield her face from the beer cans being hurled by her opponent . . . Some, lying in alcohol-induced stupors, were incapable of seeing anything. Others saw but did not care . . .

Outside an Aboriginal man with an artificial leg lay slumped unconscious against the wall ... Those on their way into the canteen stepped over or walked around him. This was standard stuff ...

The journalist must have had an exciting, and enlightening, night on Palm Island but I could easily show her an even more exciting night around some of the white wine bars in the city. However, these occurrences never seem to hit the headlines of the local newspapers.

Palm Island is, indeed, a paradise. But it was a far greater paradise before white man interfered.

Addendum

The front page of the *Weekend Australian* 28–29 November 1992:

> Palm Island, off the north Queensland coast, recorded five cases of HIV in a voluntary screening of 1,500 islanders in 1987. The most alarming aspect of the screening was the recording of three women as infected — a result which led experts to believe heterosexual spread, and not injecting drug use, was the mode of transmission.
>
> The report comes as news that an Aboriginal community which recorded one of the highest rates of HIV infection in the world no longer has a specific AIDS program.
>
> The study found that among Aborigines heterosexual transmission of HIV accounted for 21 per cent of infections compared with 4 per cent in the rest of the community.

This study of HIV infections shows the transmission rate of AIDS among Aboriginal and Torres Strait Islander people to be five times that of other Australians!

A program of awareness and education of HIV among Aborigines, called 'Turtle Dreaming', was discontinued in July 1992.